D0384535

HOW TO BE A
MATH
GENIUS

REVISED EDITION

DK LONDON
Project editor Vicky Richards   **Art editor** Chrissy Barnard
Editor Rona Skene   **US Editor** Karyn Gerhard
Managing editor Francesca Baines   **Managing art editor** Philip Letsu
Production editor Kavita Varma   **Production controller** Samantha Cross
Jacket design development manager Sophia MTT
Publisher Andrew Macintyre   **Associate publishing director** Liz Wheeler
Art director Karen Self   **Publishing director** Jonathan Metcalf

DK DELHI
Senior art editor Mahua Sharma   **Editor** Upamanyu Das
Managing editor Kingshuk Ghoshal   **Managing art editor** Sudakshina Basu
DTP designers Bimlesh Tiwary, Rakesh Kumar
Jacket designer Tanya Mehrotra

FIRST EDITION
Senior editor Francesca Baines   **Project editors** Clare Hibbert, James Mitchem
Designer Hoa Luc   **Senior art editors** Jim Green, Stefan Podhorodecki
Additional designers Dave Ball, Jeongeun Yule Park
Managing editor Linda Esposito   **Managing art editor** Diane Peyton Jones
Category publisher Laura Buller
Production editor Victoria Khroundina   **Senior production controller** Louise Minihane
Jacket editor Manisha Majithia   **Jacket designer** Laura Brim
Picture researcher Nic Dean
DK picture librarian Romaine Werblow
Publishing director Jonathan Metcalf
Associate publishing director Liz Wheeler
Art director Phil Ormerod

This American Edition, 2022
First American Edition, 2012
Published in the United States by DK Publishing
1450 Broadway, Suite 801, New York, NY 10018

A catalog record for this book is available from the Library of Congress.
ISBN 978-0-7440-5025-7

DK books are available at special discounts when purchased in
bulk for sales promotions, premiums, fundraising, or educational use.
For details, contact: DK Publishing Special Markets,
1450 Broadway, Suite 801, New York, NY 10018
SpecialSales@dk.com

For the curious
www.dk.com

This book was made with Forest
Stewardship Council ™ certified
paper—one small step in DK's
commitment to a sustainable
future. For more information, go
to www.dk.com/our-green-pledge

This book is full of puzzles and activities to boost your brain power. The activities are a lot of fun, but you should always check with an adult before you do any of them so that they know what you are doing and are sure that you are safe.

HOW TO BE A
MATH
GENIUS

Written by Dr. Mike Goldsmith
Consultant Branka Surla
Illustrated by Seb Burnett

CONTENTS

SHAPES AND SPACE

A WORLD OF MATH

The book is full of problems and puzzles for you to solve. To check the answers, turn to pages 122–125.

A WORLD OF MATH

It is impossible to imagine our world without math. We use it, often without realizing, for a whole range of activities—when we tell time, go shopping, catch a ball, or play a game. This book is all about how to get your math brain buzzing, with lots of things to do, many of the big ideas explained, and stories about how the great math brains have changed our world.

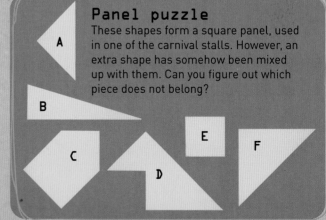

Panel puzzle
These shapes form a square panel, used in one of the carnival stalls. However, an extra shape has somehow been mixed up with them. Can you figure out which piece does not belong?

Gulp! The slide looks even steeper from the top. I wonder what speed I'll be going when I get to the bottom?

Look at me! I'm floating in the air and I've got two tongues!

One in four people are hitting a coconut. Grr! I'm making a loss.

I think I've got the angle just right... one more go and I'll win a prize.

Patterns
Many areas of math involve looking for patterns, such as how numbers repeat or how shapes behave. Often these patterns can be used to help us and inspire new ways of thinking.

Shapes
Understanding shapes and space helps us make sense of the world around us. You need to know about this area of math to create and design anything—including tricky games.

Profit margin
It costs $144 a day to run the bumper cars, accounting for wages, electricity, transportation, and so on. There are 12 bumper cars, and, on average, 60 percent of them are occupied each session. The ride is open for eight hours a day, with four sessions an hour, and each driver pays $2 per session. How much profit is the owner making?

A game of chance
Everyone loves to try to knock down a coconut—but what are your chances of success? The stall owner needs to know so he can make sure he's got enough coconuts, and to work out how much to charge. He's discovered that, on average, he has 90 customers a day, each throwing three balls, and the total number of coconuts won is 30. So what is the likelihood of you winning a coconut?

Math

brain

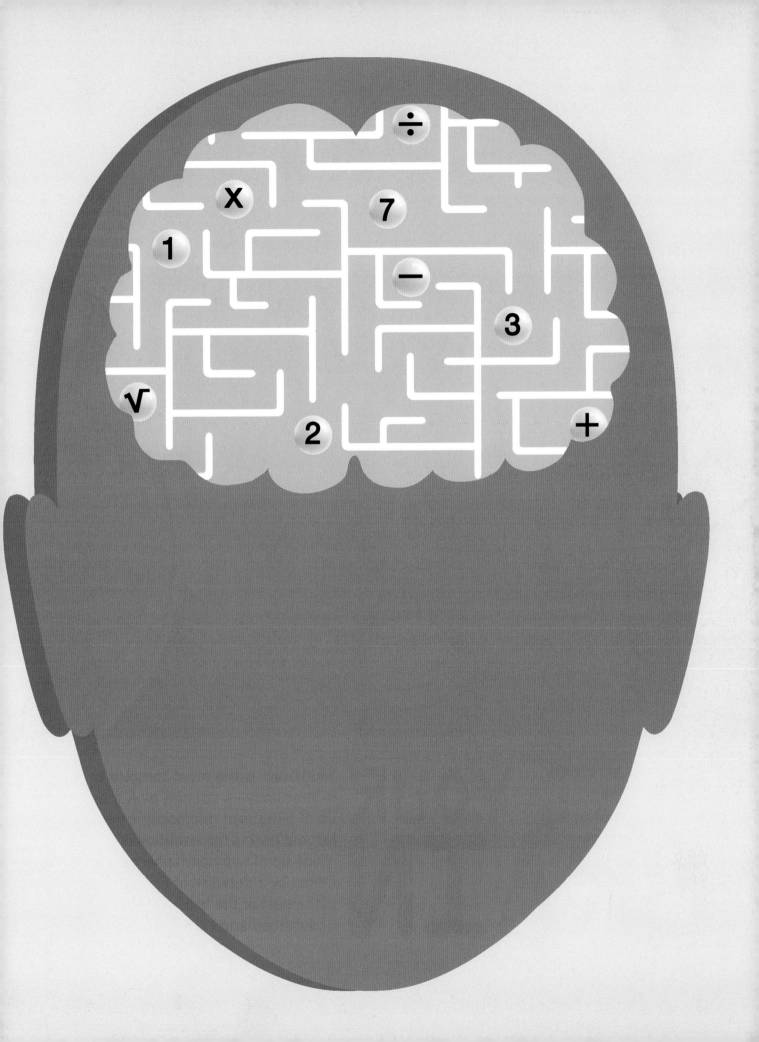

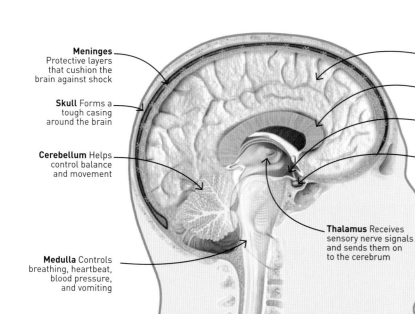

Meninges Protective layers that cushion the brain against shock

Skull Forms a tough casing around the brain

Cerebellum Helps control balance and movement

Medulla Controls breathing, heartbeat, blood pressure, and vomiting

Cerebrum Where thinking occurs and memories are stored

Corpus callosum Links the two sides of the brain

Hypothalamus Controls sleep, hunger, and body temperature

Pituitary gland Controls the release of hormones

Thalamus Receives sensory nerve signals and sends them on to the cerebrum

Looking inside
This cross-section of the skull reveals the thinking part of the brain, or cerebrum. Beneath its outer layers is the "white matter," which transfers signals between different parts of the brain.

A BRAIN OF TWO HALVES
The cerebrum has two hemispheres. Each deals mainly with the opposite side of the body—data from the right eye, for example, is handled in the brain's left side. For some functions, including math, both halves work together. For others, one half is more active than the other.

LEFT-BRAIN SKILLS
The left side of your cerebrum is responsible for the logical, rational aspects of your thinking, as well as for grammar and vocabulary. It's here that you work out the answers to calculations.

Language
The left side handles the meanings of words, but it is the right half that puts them together into sentences and stories.

Scientific thinking
Logical thinking is the job of the brain's left side, but most science also involves the creative right side.

Rational thought
Thinking and reacting in a rational way appears to be mainly a left-brain activity. It allows you to analyze a problem and find an answer.

Mathematical skills
The left brain oversees numbers and calculations, while the right processes shapes and patterns.

Writing skills
Like spoken language, writing involves both hemispheres. The right organizes ideas, while the left finds the words to express them.

Left visual cortex Processes signals from the right eye

MEET YOUR BRAIN

Your brain is the most complex organ in your body—a spongy, pink mass made up of billions of microscopic nerve cells. Its largest part is the cauliflower-like cerebrum, made up of two hemispheres, or halves, linked by a network of nerves. The cerebrum is the part of the brain where math is understood and calculations are made.

The outer surface

Thinking is carried out on the surface of the cerebrum, and the folds and wrinkles are there to make this surface as large as possible. In preserved brains, the outer layer is gray, so it is known as "gray matter."

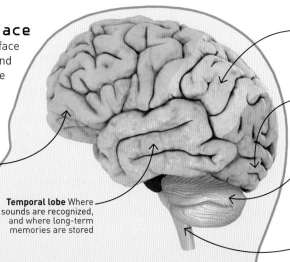

Parietal lobe Gathers together information from senses such as touch and taste

Occipital lobe Processes information from the eyes to create images

Cerebellum Tucked beneath the cerebrum's two halves, this structure coordinates the body's muscles

Spinal cord Joins the brain to the system of nerves that runs throughout the body

Right eye Collects data on light-sensitive cells that is processed in the opposite side of the brain—the left visual cortex in the occipital lobe

Right optic nerve Carries information from the right eye to the left visual cortex

Frontal lobe Vital to thought, personality, speech, and emotion

Temporal lobe Where sounds are recognized, and where long-term memories are stored

RIGHT-BRAIN SKILLS

The right side of your cerebrum is where creativity and intuition take place, and is also used to understand shapes and motion. You carry out rough calculations here, too.

Spatial skills
Understanding the shapes of objects and their positions in space is a mainly right-brain activity. It provides you your ability to visualize.

Imagination
The right side of the brain directs your imagination. Putting your thoughts into words, however, is the job of the left side of the brain.

Art
The right side of the brain looks after spatial skills. It is more active during activities such as drawing, painting, or looking at art.

Music
The brain's right side is where you appreciate music. Together with the left side, it works to make sense of the patterns that make the music sound good.

Insight
Moments of insight occur in the right side of the brain. Insight is another word for those "eureka!" moments when you see the connections between very different ideas.

Neurons and numbers

Neurons are brain cells that link up to pass electric signals to each other. Every thought, idea, or feeling that you have is the result of neurons triggering a reaction in your brain. Scientists have found that when you think of a particular number, certain neurons fire strongly.

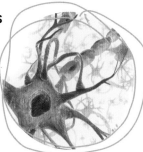

Doing the math
This brain scan was carried out on a person who was working out a series of subtraction problems. The yellow and orange areas show the parts of the brain that were producing the most electrical nerve signals. What's interesting is that areas all over the brain are active—not just one.

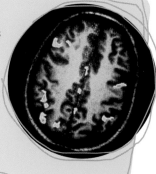

MATH SKILLS

Many parts of your brain are involved in math, with big differences between the way it works with numbers (arithmetic), and the way it grasps shapes and patterns (geometry). People who struggle in one area can often be strong in another. And sometimes there are several ways to tackle the same problem, using different math skills.

About 10 percent of people think of numbers as having colors. With some friends, try scribbling the first number between 0 and 9 that pops into your head when you think of red, then black, then blue. Do any of you get the same answers?

How do you count?
When you count in your head, do you imagine the sounds of the numbers, or the way they look? Try these two experiments and see which you find easiest.

👁 **There are four main styles of thinking, any of which can be used for learning math: seeing the words written, thinking in pictures, listening to the sounds of words, and hands-on activities.**

97...94...

88...85...

Step 1
Try counting backward in 3s from 100 in a noisy place with your eyes shut. First, try "hearing" the numbers, then visualizing them.

Step 2
Next, try both methods again while watching TV with the sound off. Which of the four exercises do you find easier?

A quick glance
Our brains have evolved to grasp key facts quickly—from just a glance at something—and also to think things over while examining them.

👁 **The part of the brain that can "see" numbers at a glance only works up to three or four, so you probably got groups less than five right. You only roughly estimate higher numbers, so are more likely to get these wrong.**

Step 1
Look at the sequences below—just glance at them briefly without counting—and write down the number of marks in each group.

Step 2
Now count the marks in each group and then check your answers. Which ones did you get right?

||||| || | |||||| || |||| ||

||||| | |||| ||| ||| |||||

Number cruncher

Your short-term memory can store a certain amount of information for a limited time. This exercise reveals your brain's ability to remember numbers. Starting at the top, read out loud a line of numbers one at a time. Then cover up the line and try to repeat it. Work your way down the list until you can't remember all the numbers.

438
7209
18546
907513
2146307
50918243
480759162
1728406395

 Most people can hold about seven numbers at a time in their short-term memory. However, we usually memorize things by saying them in our heads. Some digits take longer to say than others and this affects the number we can remember. So in Chinese, where the sounds of the words for numbers are very short, it is easier to memorize more numbers.

Eye test

This activity tests your ability to judge quantities by eye. You should not count the objects—the idea is to judge equal quantities by sight alone.

You will need:
- Pack of at least 40 small pieces of candy
- Three bowls
- Stopwatch
- A friend

Step 1
Set out the three bowls in front of you and ask your friend to time you for five seconds. When he says "go," try to divide the candy evenly between them.

Step 2
Now count up the number of candy pieces you have in each bowl. How equal were the quantities in all three?

 You'll probably be surprised how accurately you have split up the candy. Your brain has a strong sense of quantity, even though it is not thinking about it in terms of numbers.

Spot the shape

In each of these sequences, can you find the shape on the far left hidden in one of the five shapes to the right?

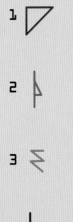

 We have a natural sense of pattern and shape. The Ancient Greek philosopher Plato discovered this a long time ago, when he showed his slaves some shape puzzles. The slaves got the answers right, even though they'd had no schooling.

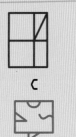

1   A B C D E
2   A B C D E
3   A B C D E
4   A B C D E

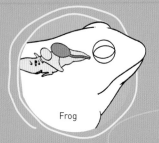

Frog

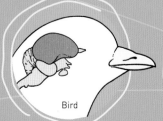

Bird

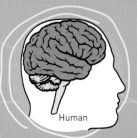

Human

Brain size and evolution

Compared with the size of the body, the human brain is much bigger than those of other animals. We also have larger brains than our apelike ancestors. A bigger brain indicates a greater capacity for learning and problem solving.

For many, the thought of learning math is daunting. But have you ever wondered where math came from? Did people make it up as they went along? The answer is yes and no. Humans—and some animals—are born with the basic rules of math, but most of it was invented.

LEARNING MATH

A sense of numbers

Over the last few years, scientists have tested babies and young children to investigate their math skills. Their findings show that we humans are all born with some knowledge of numbers.

Baby at 48 hours

Newborn babies have some sense of numbers. They can recognize that seeing 12 ducks is different from 4 ducks.

Baby at six months

In one study, a baby was shown two toys, then a screen was put up and one toy was taken away. The activity of the baby's brain revealed that it knew something was wrong, and understood the difference between one and two.

Animal antics

Many animals have a sense of numbers. A crow called Jakob could identify one among many identical boxes if it had five dots on it. And ants seem to know exactly how many steps there are between them and their nest.

ACTIVITY

Can your pet count?

All dogs can "count" up to about three. To test your dog, or the dog of a friend, let the dog see you throw one, two, or three treats somewhere out of sight. Once the dog has found the number of treats you threw, it will usually stop looking. But throw five or six treats and the dog will "lose count" and not know when to stop. It will keep on looking even after finding all the treats. Use dry treats with no smell and make sure they fall out of sight.

Sensory memory
We keep a memory of almost everything we sense, but only for half a second or so. Sensory memory can store about a dozen things at once.

Short-term memory
We can retain a handful of things (such as a few digits or words) in our memory for about a minute. After that, unless we learn them, they are forgotten.

Long-term memory
With effort, we can memorize and learn an impressive number of facts and skills. These long-term memories can stay with us for our whole lives.

How memory works

Memory is essential to math. It allows us to keep track of numbers while we work on them, and to learn tables and equations. We have different kinds of memory. As we do a math problem, for example, we remember the last few numbers only briefly (short-term memory), but we will remember how to count from 1 to 10 and so on for the rest of our lives (long-term memory).

It can help you memorize your tables if you speak or sing them. Or try writing them down, looking out for any patterns. And, of course, practice them again and again.

Child at age four

The average four-year-old can count to 10, though the numbers may not always be in the right order. He or she can also estimate larger quantities, such as hundreds. Most importantly, at four a child becomes interested in making marks on paper, showing numbers in a visual way.

I'm going to draw hundreds and hundreds of dots!

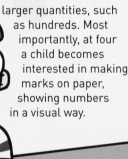

From five to nine

When a five-year-old is asked to put numbered blocks in order, he or she will tend to space the lower numbers farther apart than the higher ones. By the age of about nine, children recognize that the difference between numbers is the same—one—and space the blocks equally.

Clever Hans

Just over a century ago, there was a mathematical horse named Hans. He seemed to add, subtract, multiply, and divide, then tap out his answer with his hoof. However, Hans wasn't good at math. Unbeknownst to his owner, the horse was actually excellent at "reading" body language. He would watch his owner's face change when he had made the right number of taps, and then stop.

Prodigies

A prodigy is someone who has an incredible skill from an early age—for example, great ability in math, music, or art. India's Srinivasa Ramanujan (1887–1920) had hardly any schooling, yet became an exceptional mathematician. Prodigies have active memories that can hold masses of data at once.

BRAIN vs.

In a battle of the superpowers—brain versus machine—the human brain would be the winner! Although able to perform calculations at lightning speeds, the supercomputer, as yet, is unable to think creatively or match the mind of a genius. So, for now, we humans remain one step ahead.

Hard work

More often than not, dedication and hard work are the key to exceptional success. In 1637, a mathematician named Pierre de Fermat proposed a theorem but did not prove it. For more than three centuries, many great mathematicians tried and failed to solve the problem. Britain's Andrew Wiles became fascinated by Fermat's Last Theorem when he was 10. He finally solved it more than 30 years later in 1995.

Savants

Someone who is incredibly skilled in a specialized field is known as a savant. Born in 1979, Daniel Tammet is a British savant who can perform mind-boggling feats of calculation and memory, such as memorizing 22,514 decimal places of pi (3.141...), see pages 76–77. Tammet has synesthesia, which means he sees numbers with colors and shapes.

What about your brain?

If someone gives you some numbers to add up in your head, you keep them all "in mind" while you do the math. They are held in your short-term memory (see page 15). If you can hold more than eight numbers in your head, you've got a great math brain.

MACHINE

Computers

When they were first invented, computers were called electronic brains. It is true that, like the human brain, a computer's job is to process data and send out control signals. But, while computers can do some of the same things as brains, there are more differences than similarities between the two. Machines are not ready to take over the world just yet.

$1,200

WATSON

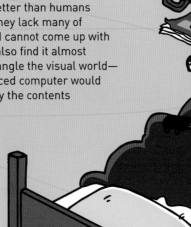

Artificial intelligence

An artificially intelligent computer is one that seems to think like a person. Even the most powerful computer has nothing like the all-round intelligence of a human being, but some can carry out certain tasks in a humanlike way. The computer system Watson, for example, learns from its mistakes, makes choices, and narrows down options. In 2011, it beat human contestants to win the quiz show *Jeopardy*.

Missing ingredient

Computers are far better than humans at calculations, but they lack many of our mental skills and cannot come up with original ideas. They also find it almost impossible to disentangle the visual world—even the most advanced computer would be at a loss to identify the contents of a messy bedroom!

Numerophobia

A phobia is a fear of something that there is no reason to be scared of, such as numbers. The most feared numbers are 4, especially in Japan and China, and 13. Fear of the number 13 even has its own name—triskaidekaphobia. Although no one is scared of all numbers, a lot of people are scared of using them!

Dyscalculia

Which of these two numbers is higher?   **76**   **46**
If you can't tell within a second, you might have dyscalculia, where the area of your brain that compares numbers does not work properly. People with dyscalculia can also have difficulty telling time. But remember, dyscalculia is very rare, so it is not a good excuse for missing the bus.

PROBLEMS WITH NUMBERS

A life without math

Although babies are born with a sense of numbers, more complicated ideas need to be taught. Most societies use and teach these mathematical ideas—but not all of them. Until recently, the Hadza people of Tanzania, for example, did not use counting, so their language had no numbers beyond 3 or 4.

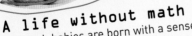

Barriers to math

German mathematician Amalie "Emmy" Noether graduated in 1907, but at first no university would offer her—or any woman—a job in mathematics. It took many years for her to get a paid job and become a professor. Despite this, she developed several groundbreaking mathematical theorems that helped scientists.

Visualizing math

Sometimes math questions sound complicated or use unfamiliar words or symbols. Drawing or visualizing (picturing in your head) can help with understanding and solving math problems. Questions about dividing shapes equally, for example, are simple enough to draw, and a rough sketch is all you need to get an idea of the answer.

Practice makes perfect

For those of us who struggle with calculations, the contestants who take part in math contests can seem like geniuses. In fact, anyone can be a math whiz if they follow the three secrets to success: practice, learning some basic calculations by heart (such as multiplication tables), and using tips and shortcuts.

A lot of people think math is tricky, and many try to avoid the subject. It is true that some people have learning difficulties with math, but they are very rare. With a little time and practice, you can soon come to grips with the basic rules of math, and once you've mastered those, then the skills are yours for life!

The 13th-century thinker Roger Bacon said, "He who is ignorant of [math] cannot know the other sciences, nor the affairs of this world."

ACTIVITY

Misleading numbers

Numbers can influence how and what you think. You need to be sure what numbers mean so they cannot be used to mislead you. Look at these two stories. You should be suspicious of the numbers in both of them—can you figure out why?

The bigger picture

In World War I, soldiers wore cloth hats, which contributed to a high number of head injuries. Better protection was required, so cloth hats were replaced by tin helmets. However, this led to a dramatic rise in head injuries. Why do you think this happened?

A useful survey?

Following a survey carried out by the Association for More Skyscrapers (AMS), it is suggested that most of the 30 parks in the city should close. The survey found that, of the three parks surveyed, two had fewer than 25 visitors all day. Can you identify four points that should make you think again about AMS's survey?

PARKS TO CLOSE!

HEAD INJURIES ON THE RISE!

Early mathematicians

People have been studying math for a long time, ever since our earliest ancestors learned to count! Later, in societies all around the world, great thinkers came up with ideas for how shapes, numbers, and equations worked. Many of these historical geniuses are still remembered for their achievements and how they paved the way for the math geniuses of today.

Aryabhata

Born in 476 CE, during the golden age of Indian math, Aryabhata was a talented mathematician and astronomer. His famous book *Aryabhatiya* describes many ideas about number systems, including how to calculate the square and cube roots of numbers. He is also known for his work on the concept of zero, later expanded upon by other Indian mathematicians such as Brahmagupta.

Euclid

This ancient Greek thinker born in 325 BCE worked mostly on math relating to shapes (geometry). In the *Elements*, a series of 13 books, he defined geometry's rules, explaining and expanding the work of earlier mathematicians. Written in clear language and set out in a logical order, the *Elements* became one of the most successful and long-lasting textbooks in history. For the next 2,000 years, it was a must-read for math students all over the world, and we still use many of his definitions and explanations today.

India's first satellite, launched in 1975, was named after Aryabhata. It stayed in Earth's orbit for almost 17 years.

Euclid precisely defined all the parts of a circle, including the circumference, the diameter, and the radius.

circumference
radius
sector
diameter
chord
segment
tangent

Hypatia studied the way a cone can be cut to produce different types of curves.

π

Zu Chongzhi calculated that the value of pi was between 3.1415926 and 3.1415927.

Hypatia

Born in about 355 CE in Alexandria, then a part of the Roman empire, Hypatia was famous during her lifetime as the world's leading mathematician and astronomer. She reworked ancient texts on geometry and number theory to make them easier to understand, and became the head of an important school of philosophy, where thinkers and students came together to work out the nature of the world around them.

Zu Chongzhi

One of many influential ancient Chinese mathematicians, Zu Chongzhi was also an inventor and a writer. He came up with many clever ways to calculate things, such as the volume of a sphere. In about 475 CE, he calculated the value of pi to 7 decimal places, which remained the most accurate approximation for almost 1,000 years!

The word "algebra" comes from the Arabic word *al-jabr*, which was part of the title of al-Khwarizmi's book *al-Kitab al-Mukhtasar fi Hisab al-Jabr wal-Muqabalah*, or *The Compendious Book on Calculation by Completion and Balancing*.

If you draw squares with sides the length of the Fibonacci numbers and put them next to each other, a spiral can be drawn through them.

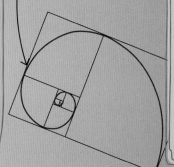

Muhammad ibn Musa al-Khwarizmi

al-Khwarizmi was born around 780 CE and lived and worked in Baghdad, then the capital of the Persian empire. He helped to transform math across the globe by introducing the Indo-Arabic number system from 0–9 that we use today. He also described the mathematical system of problem-solving that we now call algebra.

Fibonacci

Italian mathematician Fibonacci lived in the 13th century and traveled widely around the world. He introduced the Indo-Arabic number system to Europe, but is best known for discovering a sequence of numbers where each number is found by adding together the last two. This sequence is found in nature and creates spiraling patterns.

SEEING THE SOLUTION

What do you see?

The first step to sharpening the visual areas of your brain is to practice recognizing visual information. Each of these pictures is made up of the outlines of three different objects. Can you figure out what they are?

1

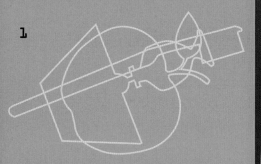

2

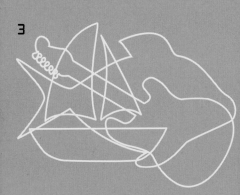

3

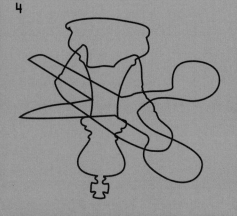

4

Thinking in 2-D

Lay out 16 matches to make five squares as shown here. By moving only two matches, can you turn the five squares into four? No matches can be removed.

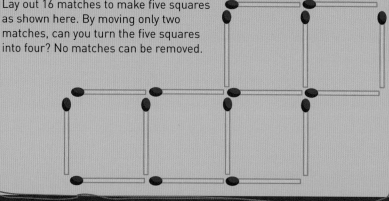

Visual sequencing

To do this puzzle, you need to visualize objects and imagine moving them around. If you placed these three tiles on top of each other, starting with the largest at the bottom, which of the four images at the bottom would you see?

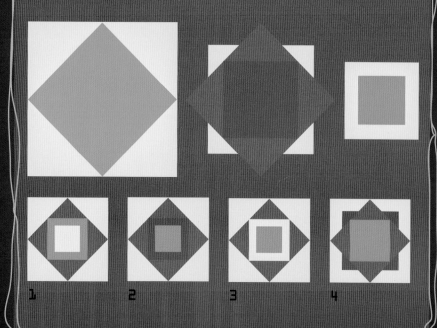

1   2   3   4

Math doesn't have to be just strings of numbers. Sometimes, it's easier to solve a math problem when you can see it as a picture—a technique known as visualization. This is because visualizing math uses different parts of the brain, which can make it easier to find logical solutions. Can you see the answers to these six problems?

3-D vision

Test your skills at mentally rotating a 3-D shape. If you folded up this shape to make a cube, which of the four options below would you see?

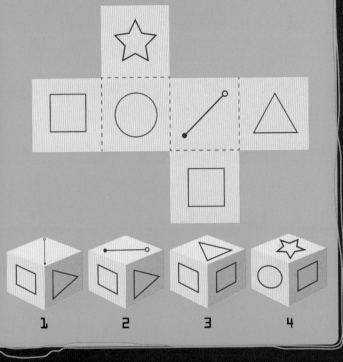

1   2   3   4

Seeing is understanding

A truly enormous snake has been spotted climbing up a tree. One half of the snake is yet to arrive at the tree. Two-thirds of the other half is wrapped around the tree trunk and 5 ft (1.5 m) of snake is hanging down from the branch. How long is the snake?

Recent studies show that playing video games develops visual awareness and increases short-term memory and attention span.

Forty percent of your brain is dedicated to seeing and processing visual material.

Illusion confusion

Optical illusions, such as this elephant, put your brain to work as it tries to make sense of an image that is in fact nonsense. Illusions also stimulate the creative side of your brain and force you to see things differently. Can you figure out how many legs this elephant has?

Inventing

numbers

LEARNING TO COUNT

We are born with some understanding of numbers, but almost everything else about math needs to be learned. The rules and skills we are taught at school had to be worked out over many centuries. Even rules that seem simple, such as which number follows 9, how to divide a cake in three, or how to draw a square, all had to be invented, long ago.

1. Fingers and tallies

People have been counting on their fingers for more than 100,000 years, keeping track of their herds, or marking the days. Since we humans have 10 fingers, we use 10 digits to count—the numerals 0, 1, 2, 3, 4, 5, 6, 7, 8, and 9. In fact, the word *digit* means "finger." When early peoples ran out of fingers, they made scratches called tallies instead. The earliest-known tally marks, on a baboon's leg bone, are 37,000 years old.

4. Egyptian math

Fractions tell us how to divide things—for example, how to share a loaf between four people. Today, we would say each person should get one quarter, or ¼. The Egyptians, working out fractions 4,500 years ago, used the eye of a god called Horus. Different parts of the eye stood for fractions, but only those produced by halving a number one or more times.

5. Greek math

Around 600 BCE, the Greeks started to develop the type of math we use today. A big breakthrough was that they didn't just have ideas about numbers and shapes—they also proved those ideas were true. Many of the laws that the Greeks proved have stood the test of time—we still rely on Euclid's ideas on shapes (geometry) and Pythagoras's work on triangles, for example.

2. From counters to numbers

The first written numbers were used in the Near East about 10,000 years ago. People there used clay counters to stand for different things: For instance, eight oval-shaped counters meant eight jars of oil. At first, the counters were wrapped with a picture, until people realized that the pictures could be used without the counters. So the picture that meant eight jars became the number 8.

3. Babylonian number rules

The place-value system (see page 31) was invented in Babylon about 5,000 years ago. This rule allowed the position of a numeral to affect its value—that's why 2,200 and 2,020 mean different things. We count in base-10, using single digits up to 9 and then double digits (10, 11, 12, and so on), but the Babylonians used base-60. They wrote their numbers as wedge-shaped marks.

The Egyptians used symbols of walking feet to represent addition and subtraction. They understood calculation by imagining a person walking right (addition) or left (subtraction) a number line.

6. New math

Gradually, the ideas of the Greeks spread far and wide, leading to new mathematical developments in the Middle East and India. In 1202, Leonardo of Pisa (an Italian mathematician also known as Fibonacci) introduced the eastern numbers and discoveries to Europe in his *Book of Calculation*. This is why our numbering system is based on an ancient Indian one.

ACTIVITY

Fizz-Buzz!

Try counting with a difference. The more people there are, the more fun it is. The idea is that you all take turns counting, except that when someone gets to a multiple of three they shout "Fizz," and when they get to a multiple of five they shout "Buzz." If a number is a multiple of both three and five, shout "Fizz-Buzz." If you get it wrong, you're out. The last remaining player is the winner.

Fizz-Buzz! Fizz-Buzz!

NUMBER SYSTEMS

The numbers we know and love today developed over many centuries from ancient systems. The earliest system of numbers that we know today is the Babylonian one, invented in Ancient Iraq at least 5,000 years ago.

Table of numbers

Ancient number systems were nearly all based on the same idea: a symbol for 1 was invented and repeated to represent small or low numbers. For larger numbers, usually starting at 10, a new symbol was invented. This, too, could be written down several times.

	1	2	3	4	5	6	7	8	9	10
Babylonian	Y	YY	YYY	YYYY	YYY	YYY	YYY	YYY	YYYY	<
Ancient Egyptian	I	II	III	IIII	IIII	III III	IIII III	IIII IIII	IIII IIII	∩
Ancient Greek	Α	Β	Γ	Δ	Ε	Ϛ	Ζ	Η	Θ	
Roman	I	II	III	IV	V	VI	VII	VIII	IX	X
Chinese	一	二	三	四	五	六	七	八	九	十
Mayan	•	••	•••	••••	—	•̣	••̣	•••̣	••••̣	=

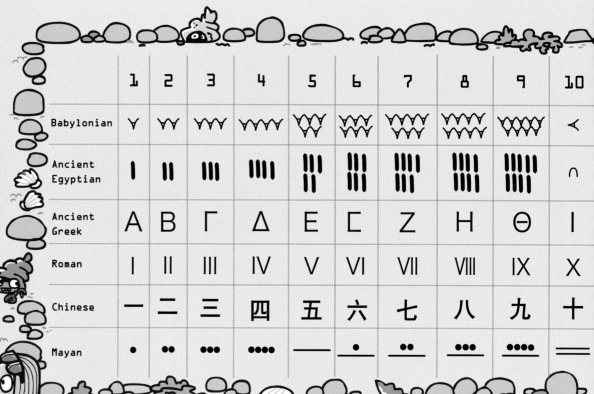

Intelligent eight-tentacled creatures would almost certainly count in base-8.

The Babylonians counted in 12s on one hand, using finger segments.

1 2 3 4 5 6 7 8 9 10 11 12

12 24 36 48 60

Base-60

The Babylonians counted in base-60. They gave their year 360 days (6 x 60). We don't know for sure how they used their hands to count. One theory is that they used a thumb to count in units up to 12 on one hand, and the fingers and thumb of the other hand to count in 12s up to a total of 60.

Their other hand kept track of the 12s—one 12 per finger or thumb.

Counting in tens

Most of us learn to count using our hands. We have 10 fingers and thumbs (digits), so we have 10 numerals (also called digits). This way of counting is known as the base-10 or decimal system, after *decem*, Latin for "ten."

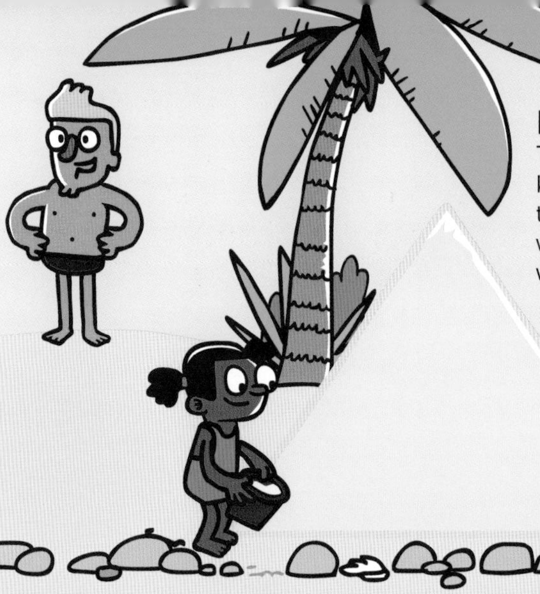

Building by numbers

The Ancient Egyptians used their mathematical knowledge for building. For instance, they knew how to work out the volume of a pyramid of any height or width. The stones used to build the Pyramids at Giza were measured so precisely that you cannot fit a credit card between them.

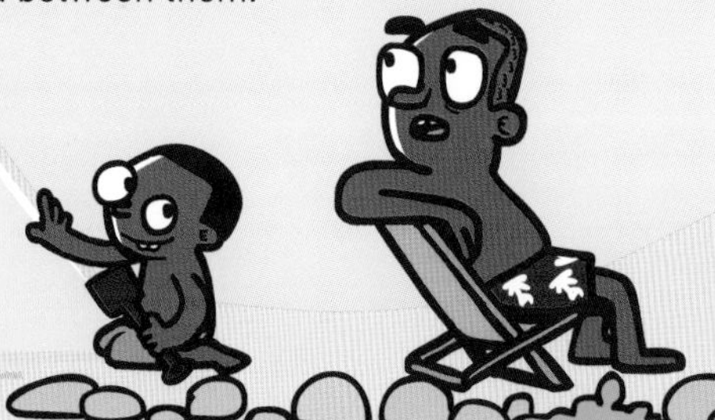

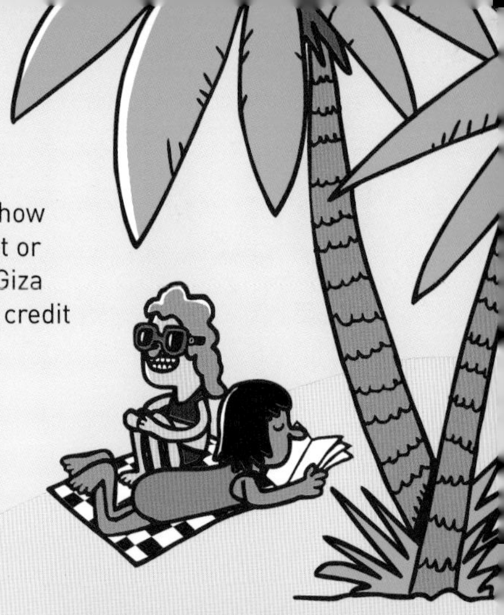

20	30	40	50	60	70	80	90	100
𒌋𒌋	𒌋𒌋𒌋	𒌋𒌋𒌋𒌋	𒌋𒌋𒌋𒌋𒌋	𒁹	𒁹𒌋	𒁹𒌋𒌋	𒁹𒌋𒌋𒌋	𒁹𒌋𒌋𒌋𒌋
𓎆𓎆	𓎆𓎆𓎆	𓎆𓎆𓎆𓎆	𓎆𓎆𓎆𓎆𓎆	𓎆𓎆𓎆𓎆𓎆𓎆	𓎆𓎆𓎆𓎆𓎆𓎆𓎆	𓎆𓎆𓎆𓎆𓎆𓎆𓎆𓎆	𓎆𓎆𓎆𓎆𓎆𓎆𓎆𓎆𓎆	𓍢
K	Λ	M	N	Ξ	O	Π	Ϙ	P
XX	XXX	XL	L	LX	LXX	LXXX	XC	C
二十	三十	四十	五十	六十	七十	八十	九十	百
𝋡 𝋠	𝋡 𝋪	𝋢 𝋠	𝋢 𝋪	𝋣 𝋠	𝋣 𝋪	𝋤 𝋠	𝋤 𝋪	𝋥 𝋠

No numbers

Imagine a world with no numbers. There would be...

- No dates, and no birthdays
- No money, no buying or selling
- No scores or times in sport, which would make things very dull
- No way of measuring distance—just keep walking until you get there!
- No measurements of heights or angles, so your house would be unstable
- No science, so no amazing inventions or technology, and no phone numbers

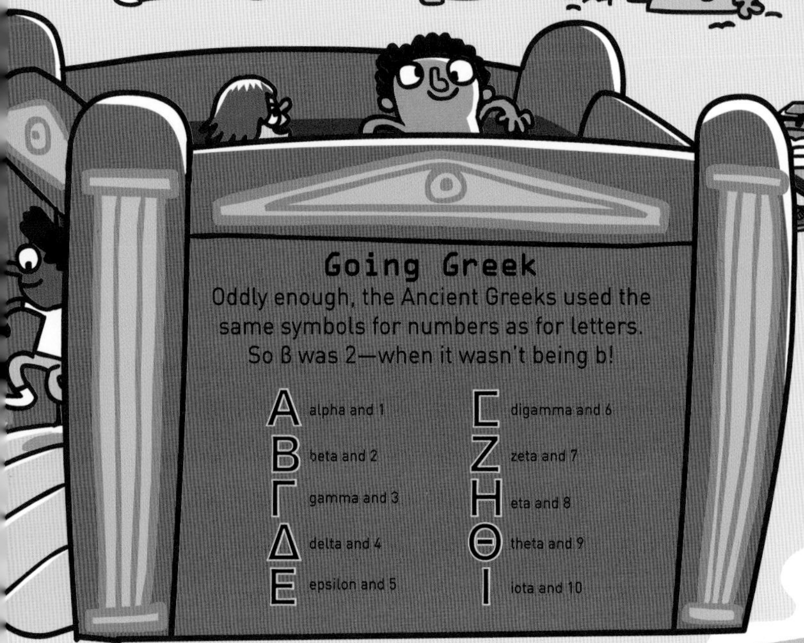

Going Greek

Oddly enough, the Ancient Greeks used the same symbols for numbers as for letters. So β was 2—when it wasn't being b!

- A alpha and 1
- B beta and 2
- Γ gamma and 3
- Δ delta and 4
- E epsilon and 5
- Ϝ digamma and 6
- Z zeta and 7
- H eta and 8
- Θ theta and 9
- I iota and 10

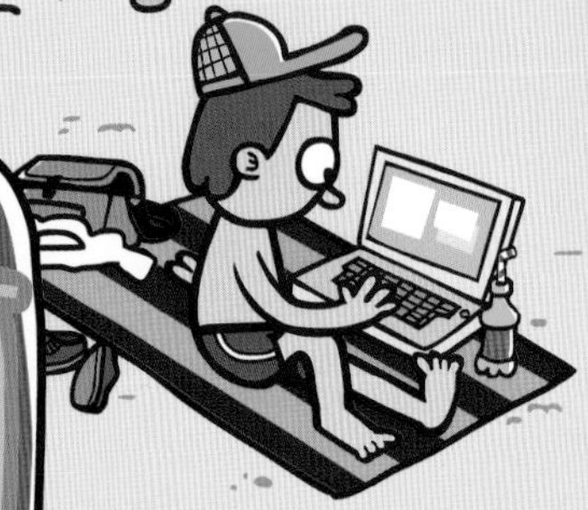

Tech talk

Computers have their own two-digit system, called binary. This is because computer systems are made of switches that have only two positions: on (1) or off (0).

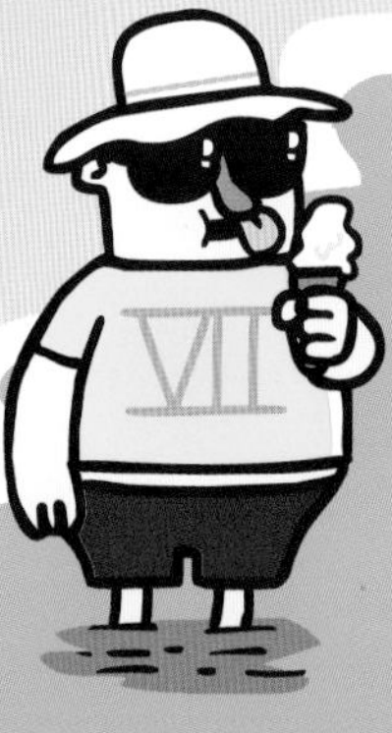

Roman numerals

In the Roman number system, if a numeral is placed before a larger one, it means it should be subtracted from it. So IV is four ("I" less than "V"). This can get tricky, though. The Roman way of writing 199, for example, is CXCIX.

BIG ZERO

Although it may seem like nothing, zero is probably the most important number of all. It was the last digit to be discovered and it's easy to see why—just try counting to zero on your fingers! Even after its introduction, this mysterious number wasn't properly understood. At first it was used as a placeholder but later became a full number.

What is zero?

Zero can mean nothing, but not always! It can also be valuable. Zero plays an important role in calculations and in everyday life. Temperature, time, and football scores can all have a value of zero—without it, everything would be very confusing!

> Any number times zero is zero.

> A number minus itself is zero.

> Is zero a number?

> Yes, but it's neither odd nor even.

> Zero isn't positive or negative.

> And you can't divide numbers by zero.

Filling the gap

An early version of zero was invented in Babylon more than 5,000 years ago. It looked like this pictogram (right) and it played one of the roles that zero does for us—it spaced out other numbers. Without it, the numbers 12, 102, and 120 would all be written in the same way: 12. But this Babylonian symbol did not have all the other useful characteristics zero has today.

Brahmagupta

Indian mathematicians were the first people to use zero as a true number, not just a placeholder. Around 650 CE, an Indian mathematician named Brahmagupta worked out how zero behaved in calculations. Even though some of Brahmagupta's answers were wrong, this was a big step forward.

Place value

In our decimal system, the value of a digit depends on its place in the number. Each place has a value of 10 times the place to the right. This place-value system only works when you have zero to "hold" the place for a value when no other digit goes in that position. So on this abacus, the 2 represents the thousands in the number, the 4 represents the hundreds, the 0 holds the place for tens, and the 6 represents the ones, making the number 2,406.

ZERO

Without zero, we wouldn't be able to tell the difference between numbers such as 11 and 101...

... and there'd be the same distance between −1 and 1 as between 1 and 2.

In a countdown, a rocket launches at "zero!"

At zero hundred hours—00:00— it's midnight.

Zero height is sea level and zero gravity exists in space.

ACTIVITY

Roman homework

The Romans had no zero and used letters to represent numbers: I was 1, V was 5, X was 10, C was 100, and D was 500 (see pages 28–29). But numbers weren't always what they seemed. For example, IX means "one less than 10," or 9. Without zero, calculations were difficult. Try adding 309 and 805 in Roman numerals (right) and you'll understand why they didn't catch on.

CCCIX
+DCCCV
_____
_____

Absolute zero

We usually measure temperatures in degrees Celsius or Fahrenheit, but scientists often use the Kelvin scale. The lowest number on this scale, 0K, is known as absolute zero. In theory, this is the lowest possible temperature in the Universe, but in reality the closest scientists have achieved are temperatures a few millionths of a Kelvin warmer than absolute zero.

Temperature		
212°F (100°C)	373K	Water boils
32°F (0°C)	273K	Water freezes
−108°F (−78°C)	195K	CO_2 freezes (dry ice)
−459°F (−273°C)	0K	Absolute zero

Pythagoras

Pythagoras is perhaps the most famous mathematician of the ancient world, and is best known for his theorem on right-angled triangles. Ever curious about the world around him, Pythagoras learned much on his travels. He studied music in Egypt and may have been the first to invent a musical scale.

Early travels

Born around 570 BCE on the Greek island of Samos, it is thought that Pythagoras traveled to Egypt, Babylon (modern-day Iraq), and perhaps even India in search of knowledge. When he was in his forties, he finally settled in Croton, a town in Italy that was under Greek control.

The school of Pythagoras was made up of an inner circle of mathematicians, and a larger group who came to listen to them speak. According to some accounts, Pythagoras did his work in the peace and quiet of a cave.

Pythagoras thought of odd numbers as male, and even numbers as female.

For Pythagoras, the most perfect shape-making number was 10, its dots forming a triangle known as the tetractys.

Prestigious pupils

In Croton, Pythagoras formed a school where mainly math but also religion and mysticism were studied. Women and men were treated as equals in the school and Pythagoras is thought to have mentored and married Theano—possibly the first known woman mathematician and also a philosopher. Little is known about her life, but historians believe she published several works, likely to do with the geometrical concept of the golden ratio.

Pythagorean theorem

Pythagoras's name lives on today in his famous theorem. It says that, in a right-angled triangle, the square of the hypotenuse (the longest side, opposite the right angle) is equal to the sum of the squares of the other two sides. The theorem can be written mathematically as $a^2 + b^2 = c^2$.

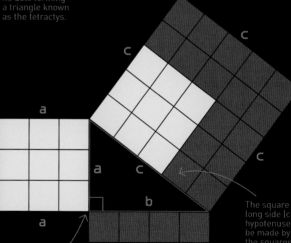

The triangle's right angle is opposite the longest side, the hypotenuse.

The square of the long side (c), the hypotenuse, can be made by adding the squares of the other two sides (a and b).

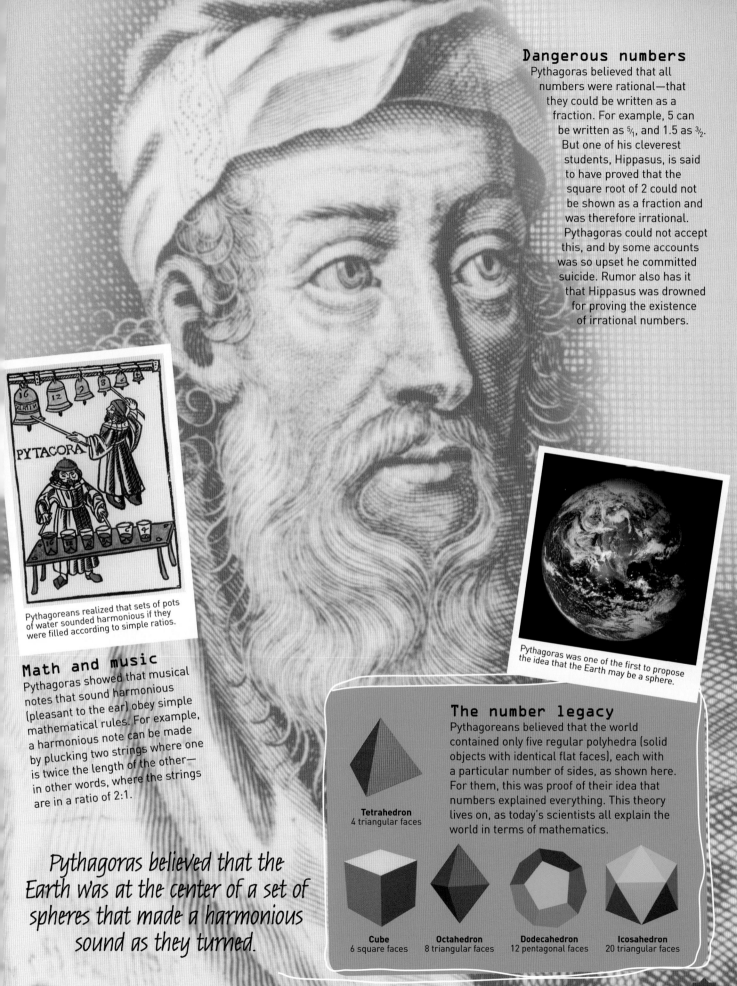

Dangerous numbers

Pythagoras believed that all numbers were rational—that they could be written as a fraction. For example, 5 can be written as $^5/_1$, and 1.5 as $^3/_2$. But one of his cleverest students, Hippasus, is said to have proved that the square root of 2 could not be shown as a fraction and was therefore irrational. Pythagoras could not accept this, and by some accounts was so upset he committed suicide. Rumor also has it that Hippasus was drowned for proving the existence of irrational numbers.

Pythagoreans realized that sets of pots of water sounded harmonious if they were filled according to simple ratios.

Pythagoras was one of the first to propose the idea that the Earth may be a sphere.

Math and music

Pythagoras showed that musical notes that sound harmonious (pleasant to the ear) obey simple mathematical rules. For example, a harmonious note can be made by plucking two strings where one is twice the length of the other—in other words, where the strings are in a ratio of 2:1.

Pythagoras believed that the Earth was at the center of a set of spheres that made a harmonious sound as they turned.

The number legacy

Pythagoreans believed that the world contained only five regular polyhedra (solid objects with identical flat faces), each with a particular number of sides, as shown here. For them, this was proof of their idea that numbers explained everything. This theory lives on, as today's scientists all explain the world in terms of mathematics.

Tetrahedron
4 triangular faces

Cube
6 square faces

Octahedron
8 triangular faces

Dodecahedron
12 pentagonal faces

Icosahedron
20 triangular faces

THINKING OUTSIDE THE BOX

Some problems can't be solved by working through them step-by-step, and need to be looked at in a different way—sometimes we can simply "see" the answer. This intuitive way of figuring things out is one of the most difficult parts of the brain's workings to explain. Sometimes, seeing an answer is easier if you try to approach the problem in an unusual way—this is called lateral thinking.

1. Changing places
You are running in a race and overtake the person in second place. What position are you in now?

2. Pop!
How can you stick 10 pins into a balloon without popping it?

3. What are the odds?
You meet a mother with two children. She tells you that one of them is a boy. What is the probability that the other is also a boy?

4. Sister act
A mother and father have two daughters who were born on the same day of the same month of the same year, but are not twins. How are they related to each other?

5. In the money
You have two identical money bags. One is filled with small coins. The other is filled with coins that are twice the size and value of the others. Which of the bags is worth more?

6. How many?
If 10 children can eat 10 bananas in 10 minutes, how many children would be needed to eat 100 bananas in 100 minutes?

7. Left or right?
A left-handed glove can be changed into a right-handed one by looking at it in a mirror. Can you think of another way?

8. The lonely man
There was a man who never left his house. The only visitor he had was someone delivering supplies every two weeks. One dark and stormy night, he lost control of his senses, turned off all the lights, and went to sleep. The next morning it was discovered that his actions had resulted in the deaths of several people. Why?

9. A cut above

A New York City hairdresser recently said that he would rather cut the hair of three Canadians than one New Yorker. Why would he say this?

10. Half full

Three of the glasses below are filled with orange juice and the other three are empty. By touching just one glass, can you arrange it so that the full and empty glasses alternate?

11. At a loss

A man buys sacks of rice for $1 a pound from American farmers and then sells them for $0.05 a pound in India. As a result, he becomes a millionaire. How?

12. Whodunnit?

Acting on an anonymous phone call, the police raid a house to arrest a suspected murderer. They don't know what he looks like but they know his name is John and that he is inside the house. Inside they find a carpenter, a truck driver, a mechanic, and a fireman playing poker. Without hesitation or communication of any kind, they immediately arrest the fireman. How do they know they have their man?

13. Frozen!

You are trapped in a cabin on a cold snowy mountain with the temperature falling and night coming on. You have a matchbox containing just a single match. You find the following things in the cabin. What do you light first?

- A candle
- A gas lamp
- A windproof lantern
- A wood fire with fire starters
- A signal flare to attract rescuers

14. Crash!

A plane takes off from London headed for Japan. After a few hours there is an engine malfunction and the plane crashes on the Italian/Swiss border. Where do they bury the survivors?

FRAGILE

16. Home

A man built a rectangular house with all four sides facing south. One morning he looked out of the window and spotted a bear. What color was it?

15. Leave it to them

Some children are raking leaves in their street. They gather seven piles at one house, four piles at another, and five piles at another. When the children put all the piles together, how many will they have?

NUMBER PATTERNS

Thousands of years ago, some Ancient Greeks thought of numbers as having shapes, perhaps because different shapes can be made by arranging particular numbers of objects. Sequences of numbers can make patterns, too.

Square numbers

If a particular number of objects can be arranged to make a square with no gaps, that number is called a square number. You can also make a square number by "squaring" a number—which means multiplying a number by itself: 1 x 1 = 1, 2 x 2 = 4, 3 x 3 = 9, and so on.

16 objects can be arranged to make a 4 x 4 square.

1   4   9   16   25

$$1^2 = 1$$
$$11^2 = 121$$
$$111^2 = 12321$$
$$1111^2 = 1234321$$
$$11111^2 = 123454321$$
$$111111^2 = 12345654321$$

The magic ones

By squaring numbers made of nothing but ones, you can make all the other digits appear—eventually! Stranger still, those digits appear in numbers that read the same whether you look at them forward or backward.

Something odd

The first five square numbers are 1, 4, 9, 16, and 25. Work out the difference between each pair in the sequence (the difference between 1 and 4 is 3, for example). Write your answers out in order. Can you spot an odd pattern?

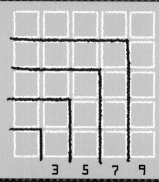

3   5   7   9

Triangular numbers

If you can make an equilateral triangle (a triangle with sides of equal length) from a particular number of objects, that number is known as triangular. You can make triangular numbers by adding numbers that are consecutive (next to each other): 0 + 1 = 1, 0 + 1 + 2 = 3, 0 + 1 + 2 + 3 = 6, and so on. Many Ancient Greek mathematicians were fascinated by triangular numbers, but we don't use them much today, except to admire the pattern!

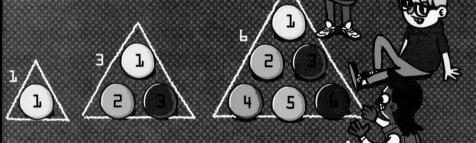

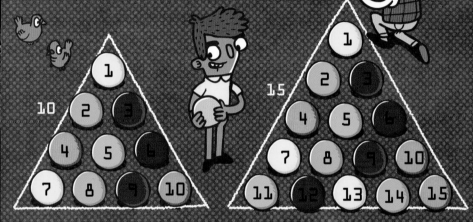

Cubic numbers

If a number of objects, such as building blocks, can be assembled to make a cube shape, then that number is called a cubic number. Cubic numbers can also be made by multiplying a number by itself twice. For example, 2 x 2 x 2 = 8.

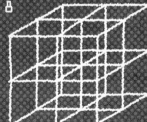

1

8

27

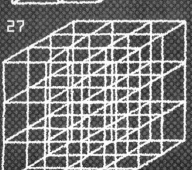

Prison break

At the prison, 20 prisoners are locked in 20 cells. The 20 prison guards looking after them have a strange way of locking up. The first guard unlocks all the cells. The second guard then locks every second door (2, 4, 6, etc.). The third turns the key in every third door, locking it if it is unlocked and unlocking it if it is locked. The fourth guard turns the key in every fourth door, and so on until all 20 guards have left. Which cells remain open allowing the prisoners to escape? Can you spot a pattern in these numbers?

Shaking hands

A group of three friends meet and everyone shakes hands with everyone else once. How many handshakes are there in total? Try drawing this out, with a dot for each person and lines between them for handshakes. Now work out the handshakes for groups of four, five, or six people. Can you spot a pattern?

A perfect solution?

The numbers 1, 2, 3, and 6 all divide into the number 6, so we call them its factors. A perfect number is one that's the sum of its factors (other than itself). So, 1 + 2 + 3 = 6, making 6 a perfect number. Can you figure out the next perfect number?

CALCULATION TIPS

Mathematicians use all kinds of tricks and shortcuts to reach their answers quickly. Most can be learned easily and are worth learning to save time and impress your friends and teachers.

To work out 9 x 9, bend down your ninth finger.

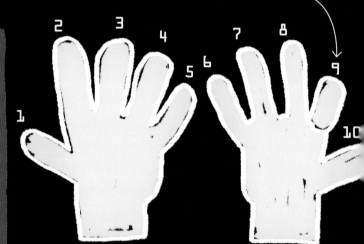

Multiplication tips

Mastering your times tables is an essential math skill, but these tips will also help you out in a pinch:

• To quickly multiply by 4, simply double the number, and then double it again.

• If you have to multiply a number by 5, find the answer by halving the number and then multiplying it by 10. So 24 x 5 would be 24 ÷ 2 = 12, then 12 x 10 = 120.

• An easy way to multiply a number by 11 is to take the number, multiply it by 10, and then add the original number once more.

• To multiply large numbers when one is even, halve the even number and double the other one. Repeat if the halved number is still even. So, 32 x 125 is the same as 16 x 250, which is the same as 8 x 500, which is the same as 4 x 1,000. They all equal 4,000.

Multiply by 9 with your hands

Here's a trick that will make multiplying by 9 a breeze.

Step 1

Hold your hands face up in front of you. Find out what number you need to multiply by 9 and bend the corresponding finger. So to work out 9 x 9, turn down your ninth finger.

Step 2

Take the number of fingers on the left side of the bent finger, and combine (not add) it with the one on the right. For example, if you bent your ninth finger, you'd combine the number of fingers on the left, 8, with the number of fingers on the right, 1. So you'd have 81 (9 x 9 is 81).

Alex Lemaire

With plenty of practice, people can solve amazing math problems without a calculator. In 2007, French mathematician Alex Lemaire worked out the number that, if multiplied by itself 13 times, gives a particular 200 digit number. He gave the correct answer in 70 seconds!

Division tips

There are lots of tips that can help speed up your division:

- To find out if a number is divisible by 3, add up the digits. If they add up to a multiple of 3, the number will be divisible by 3. For instance, 5,394 must be divisible by 3 because 5 + 3 + 9 + 4 = 21, and 21 is divisible by 3.

- A number is divisible by 6 if it's divisible by 3 and the last digit is even.

- A number is divisible by 9 if all the digits add up to a multiple of 9. For instance, 201,915 must be divisible by 9 because 2 + 0 + 1 + 9 + 1 + 5 = 18, and 18 is divisible by 9.

- To find out if a number is divisible by 11, start with the digit on the left, subtract the next digit from it, then add the next, subtract the next, and so on. If the answer is 0 or 11, then the original number is divisible by 11. For example, 35,706 is divisible by 11 because 3 − 5 + 7 − 0 + 6 = 11.

In Asia, children use an abacus (a frame of bars of beads) to add and subtract faster than an electronic calculator.

Calculating a tip

If you need to leave a 15 percent tip after a meal at a restaurant, here's an easy shortcut: Just work out 10 percent (divide the number by 10), then add that number to half its value, and you have your answer.

$$10\% \text{ of } \$35 = \$3.50$$
$$\$3.50 \div 2 = \$1.75$$
$$\$3.50 + \$1.75 = \$5.25$$

Fast squaring

If you need to square a two-digit number that ends in 5, just multiply the first digit by itself plus 1, then put 25 on the end. So to square 15, do: 1 x (1 + 1) = 2, then attach 25 to give 225. This is how you can work out the square of 25:

$$2 \times (2+1) = 6$$
$$6 \text{ and } 25 = 625$$

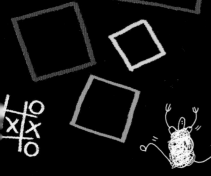

Beat the clock

Test your powers of mental arithmetic in this game against the clock. It's more fun if you play with a group of friends.

Step 1

First, one of you must choose two of the following numbers: 25, 50, 75, 100. Next, someone else selects four numbers between 1 and 10. Now get a friend to pick a number between 100 and 999. Write this down next to the six smaller numbers.

Step 2

You all now have two minutes to add, subtract, multiply, or divide your chosen numbers—which you can use only once—to get as close as possible to the big number. The winner is the person with the exact or closest number.

Archimedes

Archimedes was probably the greatest mathematician of the ancient world. Unlike most of the others, he was a highly practical person too, using his math skills to build all kinds of contraptions, including some extraordinary war machines.

When Archimedes was in Egypt, he would have studied in the library in Alexandria, the greatest library of the ancient world.

On discovering how to measure volume, Archimedes is said to have jumped out of his bath and run naked down the street, shouting, "Eureka!" (I've found it!).

Early life

Archimedes was born in Syracuse, Sicily, in 287 BCE. As a young man he traveled to Egypt and worked with mathematicians there. According to one story, when Archimedes returned home to Syracuse, he heard that the Egyptian mathematicians were claiming some of his discoveries as their own. To catch them, he sent them some calculations with errors in them. The Egyptians claimed these new discoveries too, but were caught when people discovered that the calculations were wrong.

Eureka!

Archimedes' most famous discovery came about when the king asked him to check if his crown was pure gold. To answer this, he had to measure the crown's volume, but how? Stepping into a full bath, Archimedes realized that the water that spilled from the tub could be measured to find out the volume of his body—or a crown.

Ingenious inventions

Archimedes is credited with building the world's first planetarium—a machine that shows the motions of the Sun, Moon, and planets. One thing he didn't invent, despite it bearing his name, is the Archimedean screw. It is more likely that he introduced this design for a water pump, having seen it in Egypt.

An Archimedean screw is a cylinder with a screw inside. The screw raises water as it turns.

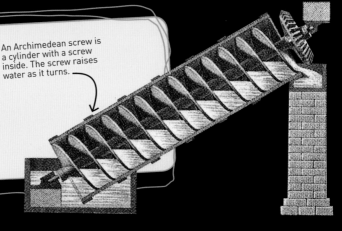

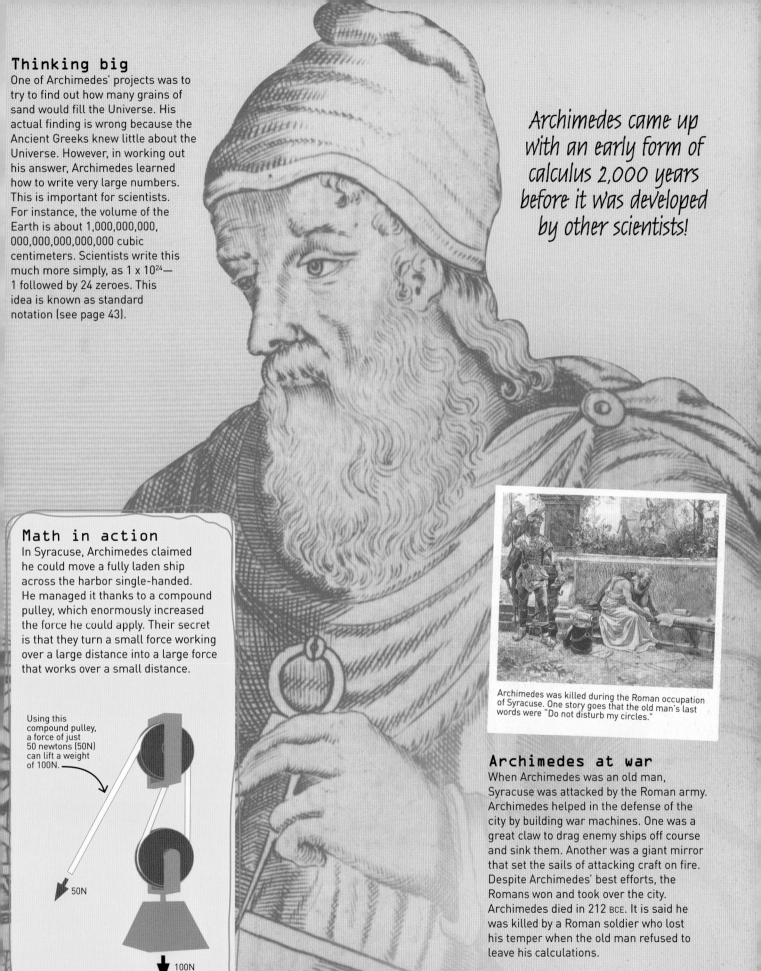

Thinking big

One of Archimedes' projects was to try to find out how many grains of sand would fill the Universe. His actual finding is wrong because the Ancient Greeks knew little about the Universe. However, in working out his answer, Archimedes learned how to write very large numbers. This is important for scientists. For instance, the volume of the Earth is about 1,000,000,000, 000,000,000,000,000 cubic centimeters. Scientists write this much more simply, as 1×10^{24}— 1 followed by 24 zeroes. This idea is known as standard notation (see page 43).

Archimedes came up with an early form of calculus 2,000 years before it was developed by other scientists!

Math in action

In Syracuse, Archimedes claimed he could move a fully laden ship across the harbor single-handed. He managed it thanks to a compound pulley, which enormously increased the force he could apply. Their secret is that they turn a small force working over a large distance into a large force that works over a small distance.

Using this compound pulley, a force of just 50 newtons (50N) can lift a weight of 100N.

50N

100N

Archimedes was killed during the Roman occupation of Syracuse. One story goes that the old man's last words were "Do not disturb my circles."

Archimedes at war

When Archimedes was an old man, Syracuse was attacked by the Roman army. Archimedes helped in the defense of the city by building war machines. One was a great claw to drag enemy ships off course and sink them. Another was a giant mirror that set the sails of attacking craft on fire. Despite Archimedes' best efforts, the Romans won and took over the city. Archimedes died in 212 BCE. It is said he was killed by a Roman soldier who lost his temper when the old man refused to leave his calculations.

MATH THAT MEASURES

We use measurements every day, from checking the time to buying food and choosing clothes. The idea is always the same—to find out how many units (such as inches or pounds) there are in the thing you want to measure, by using some kind of measuring device.

Measuring up

Anything that can be expressed in numbers can be measured, from the age of the Universe to the mass of your mom. Once you have measurements, you can use them for lots of things, such as building a car or explaining why the Sun shines, and they can play a vital part in forensics to help solve crimes.

Line of attack

Forensic scientists use all kinds of measurements to get a picture of the crime. The position of evidence is noted and angles are measured to work out the criminal's actions, the paths of moving objects, and whether witnesses could have seen what they claim from where they were standing.

Standard units

Every kind of measurement has at least one unit, usually more. It's vital that everyone knows exactly what these are, so seven basic units, called standard units, have been agreed on internationally (see below). If units are confused, accidents can happen. In 1999, a Mars probe crashed into the planet because it was programmed in metric units, such as meters and kilograms, but the controllers sent instructions in inches and pounds.

Unit name (symbol)	Measures
meter (m)	Length
kilogram (kg)	Mass
second (s)	Time
ampere (A)	Electric current
kelvin (K)	Thermodynamic temperature
mole (mol)	Amount of substance
candela (cd)	Luminous intensity

Matching prints

Everyone has different fingerprints. The police can measure the shapes of the lines in a fingerprint found at a crime scene and see if they match the measurements of the fingerprint of a suspect.

Under pressure
The behavior of your body, such as heart rate and blood pressure, can also be measured. Lie detectors take measurements like this, but unusual activity may not always be caused by lying, so cannot be used as evidence.

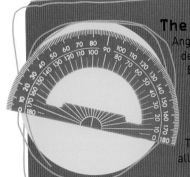

The right angle
Angles are usually measured in degrees, a unit invented in Ancient Babylon (now Iraq). Stargazers wanted to describe the positions of stars in the night sky, so they divided a circle into 360 portions, each of which is one degree. Today, we use degrees to measure all kinds of angles.

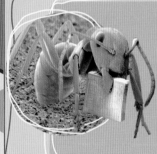

Leave no trace
Wherever you go, you leave traces of yourself behind— a hair, sweat, a drop of blood, or particles of soil from your shoes. Forensic scientists can measure and match the chemicals in tiny samples of trace evidence to link a person to a crime.

Tiny units
1 micrometer = 10^{-6} m
1 nanometer = 10^{-9} m
1 picometer = 10^{-12} m
1 femtometer = 10^{-15} m
1 yoctometer = 10^{-24} m

This magnified ant has a microchip 10^{-3} m (1 mm) wide in its jaws.

Scientific notation
To measure very small or large things, we can either use fractions of metric units, like those above, or special units, like those below. To avoid lots of zeros and save space, large or small numbers are written in scientific notation, which uses powers of 10. So two million is 2×10^6, while one-millionth is 1×10^{-6}.

Huge units
Astronomical unit = 1.5×10^{11} m
Light-year = 9.46×10^{15} m
Parsec = 3×10^{16} m
Kiloparsec = 3×10^{19} m
Megaparsec= 3×10^{22} m

Our galaxy, the Milky Way, is 100,00 light-years, or 10^{21} m, across.

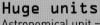

If the shoe fits...
Measuring footprints can reveal more than the wearer's shoe size. The person's height, weight, and whether they were running or walking can be determined too. The pattern of the sole can be compared with suspect's shoes.

HOW BIG?
HOW FAR?

In this high-tech world, full of gizmos and gadgets, you rarely have to figure out anything for yourself anymore. But there's something very satisfying about solving a problem using your wits and a few simple calculations. Here are some interesting tips and challenges to put your mind to.

The Egyptians used the hand to measure small sizes

Digit—the breadth of a finger

Span

Palm

Inch—from tip to first joint of the thumb

Foot

The Romans measured long distances using paces and feet

Pace—the distance one foot travels from back to front, so two steps

From hand to foot

Imagine you are washed up on an island with nothing but the clothes on your back and some treasure. You want to bury the treasure so you can explore the island and, with luck, find help. The softest area of sand is some distance from a lone palm tree—how can you measure the distance to the spot so that you know where to find it again? The solution is the world's first measuring instrument, the human body, which is how the Ancient Egyptians and Romans did it. The flaw with this system, of course, is that people come in all shapes and sizes, so measurements are not going to be the same.

Watch the shadow

Have you ever wondered how tall your house or a favorite tree is? On a sunny day, it's easy enough to find out by using your shadow as a guide. The best time to do this is just before the Sun is at an angle of 45° in the sky.

You will need:
• A sunny day
• A tape measure

Step 1
On a sunny day, stand in a good spot next to the object you want to measure, with the Sun at your back. Lie on the ground and mark your height—the top of your head and the bottom of your feet.

Step 2
Stand on the mark for your feet and wait. Watch your shadow. When the Sun is at 45° your shadow will equal your height.

If you can't wait until the length of your shadow is the same as your height, work out the scale of the shadow in relation to your height—is it half your height, for example? Then you just need to double the measurements.

Step 3
Rush over to the tall object and measure its shadow, which will also be equal to its height.

Time a storm

There's a thunder storm on the horizon, but how far away is it and is it coming or going? Here's how to find out.

Step 1

Watch out for the lightning and listen for thunder. When you see a flash of lightning, start counting the seconds until the thunder rumbles. You can do this using the second hand on your watch, but if you don't have one, just count the seconds.

Step 2

Then take your total number of seconds and divide it by five to get the distance in miles (by three to get the distance in kilometers). So if you count 15 seconds, the storm is 3 miles (5 km) away.

To count seconds without a watch, use a long word to help keep an accurate rhythm. For example, "One Mississippi, two Mississippi..." and so on. Other good words are chimpanzee and elephant.

Measure the Earth

More than 2,000 years ago, the Ancient Greek mathematician Eratosthenes measured the size of the Earth and got it almost exactly right. Here's how he did it, but this time, see if you can work out the answer.

Step 1

Eratosthenes came across a well in Syene in the south of Egypt where a beam of light shone right down into the well, and reflected back off the water at the bottom, at only one time each year—noon on midsummer's day. He realized this meant the Sun was directly overhead.

The Sun was directly above the well

Beams of light shone straight down the well

The water at the bottom of the well acted like a mirror, reflecting the light back up

Step 2

Then Eratosthenes discovered that on midsummer's day in Alexandria in the north of Egypt, the Sun strikes the ground at a slight angle, casting a shadow. Drawing a triangle, he worked out that the angle of the Sun's rays was 7.2°.

7.2°

Syene   Alexandria

7.2°

Step 3

You know the Earth is round, so imagine two lines, one vertical, the other at an angle of 7.2°, extending to the center of the Earth. You know that a circle has 360°, so divide 360 by 7.2 to find out what fraction this slice is of the whole Earth. If the distance between Syene and Alexandria is 500 miles (800 km), can you calculate the Earth's circumference?

THE SIZE OF THE PROBLEM

There's almost nothing you can't measure, from the everyday to the extreme. Here are some scary scales—the Fujita, Torino, and hobo—so you'll know if you should run, duck, or hold your nose!

Stand back!

Volcanic explosivity is measured on a scale of 1 to 8 according to how much material is spewed out, how high it goes, and how long the eruption lasts. A value of 0 is given to nonexplosive eruptions, 1 is gentle, then every increase of 1 on the scale indicates an explosion 10 times as powerful.

0 : Effusive—**Kilauea** (continuing)
1 : Gentle—**Stromboli** (continuing)
2 : Explosive—**Mount Sinabung** 2010
3 : Severe—**Soufrière Hills** 1995
4 : Cataclysmic—**Eyjafjallajökull** 2010
5 : Paroxysmal—**Mount Vesuvius** 79 CE
6 : Colossal—**Krakatoa** 1883
7 : Super-colossal—**Thera** c.1600 BCE
8 : Mega-colossal—**Yellowstone** 640,000 YEARS AGO

Armageddon?

Asteroids aren't just in the movies—the Solar System is full of them! Astronomers use the Torino scale to measure the threat of one hitting Earth and causing destruction. A 0 means we're all going to be OK, a 5 is a slightly alarming close encounter, and a 10 means we're all doomed (unless you're in a movie)!

Shhhhh!

Sound is tricky to measure. It can be high or low in pitch (measured in hertz) as well as loud or soft. Its loudness is related to its power, which is measured in decibels (dB). The softest sound audible to humans is 0 dB, typical speech is 55–65 dB, and a jet engine 100 ft (30 m) away is 140 dB. Any sound more than 120 dB can damage your hearing.

Stubble scale

One beard-second is the length a man's beard grows in one second: 5 nanometers (0.000005 mm). It's such a tiny measurement, it's only used by scientists.

Twister

The Fujita scale is used to rate the intensity of tornadoes, based on wind speeds and how much damage they cause. An F-0 might damage the chimney, an F-3 will take the roof off, and an F-5 will blow your house away!

F-0 : 40–72 mph (64–116 km/h)—**Light damage**

F-1 : 73–112 mph (117–180 km/h)—**Moderate damage**

F-2 : 113–157 mph (181–253 km/h)—**Significant damage**

F-3 : 158–206 mph (254–332 km/h)—**Severe damage**

F-4 : 207–260 mph (333–418 km/h)—**Devastating damage**

F-5 : 261–318 mph (419–512 km/h)—**Incredible damage**

Big as a barn

A barn sounds big, but in physics one barn is the size of the nucleus of a uranium atom, which is very, very small!

Watch out!

If you're out and about in snowy mountain regions, you need to know about the avalanche danger scale. This uses color-coded signs, and works like traffic signals. Green means good to go and low risk. Yellow and orange mean medium risk, so take care. Red and black mean stay at home or you'll cause an avalanche yourself!

Hot, hot, hot!

The spicy heat of chili peppers is measured on the Scoville scale, which ranges from 0 (mild) to 1 million (explosive). Beware!

0 : Bell pepper
2,500 : Jalapeño
30,000 : Cayenne pepper
200,000 : Habanero pepper
1,000,000 : Naga Jolokia

Mouthful

The official amount of food in a mouthful is 1 oz (28 ml). But who would want a carefully measured mouthful of food?

Pee-ew!

You can even measure how bad something smells using the hobo scale, which runs from 0 to 100.

0 : No smell
13 : An average fart
50 : So bad it will make you vomit
100 : Lethal

Horsepower

Horsepower is the unit used to measure the power or output of engines or motors. The scale dates from a time when people wanted to compare the power of the newly invented steam engine with that of horses. The idea stuck and we still rate cars and trucks in "horsepower" today.

Magic

numbers

SEEING SEQUENCES

Math is the search for patterns—patterns of numbers, of shapes, of anything. Wherever there's any kind of pattern, there is usually something interesting going on, such as a meaning or a structure. A number sequence obeys a rule or pattern—the fun is in figuring out the pattern.

Types of sequences

There are two main types of sequence: arithmetic and geometric. In an arithmetic sequence, the gap between each number (called a "term") is the same, so the sequence 1, 2, 3, 4... is arithmetic (there is a gap of 1 between each term). A geometric sequence is one where there the terms increase or decrease by a fixed ratio, for example 1, 2, 4, 8, 16... (the number double each time), is a geometric sequence.

5, 10, 15, 20

In an arithmetic sequence, the numbers increase by jumps that are the same size.

1, 2, 4, 8, 16

In a geometric sequence, the numbers increase by jumps that change size.

What comes next?

Figuring out the pattern of a sequence is useful because you can then see what's going to come next. For example, Thomas Malthus, a 19th-century economist, decided that the amount of food grown on Earth increased over time in an arithmetic sequence. Population, however, increases geometrically. Malthus decided this meant that food supply could not keep up with population, so if things continued this way, one day we would run out of food.

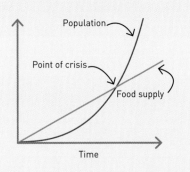

Population

Point of crisis

Food supply

Time

ACTIVITY

What's the pattern?

Can you see the pattern in the sequences below and figure out what the next term will be for each one?

A 1, 100, 10,000...

B 3, 7, 11, 15, 19...

C 64, 32, 16...

D 1, 4, 9, 16, 25, 36...

E 11, 9, 12, 8, 13, 7...

F 1, 2, 4, 7, 11, 16...

G 1, 3, 6, 10, 15...

H 2, 6, 12, 20, 30...

In 1965, a computer company expert, Gordon E. Moore, predicted that the power of computers would double every two years. He was right!

Each number in the sequence is the sum of the two previous ones.

1, 1, 2, 3, 5, 8, 13, 21, 34, 55...

Fibonacci sequence

One of the best-known number patterns is the Fibonacci sequence, named after the Italian mathematician who found it. Each number in the sequence is the sum of the two previous numbers. This pattern is found everywhere in nature, and particularly plants, in the number of petals on flowers, the arrangement of seeds, and the branching of trees.

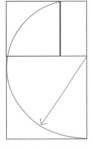

Many flowers have numbers of petals from the Fibonacci sequence.

The symbol for phi Φ

The golden ratio

The Fibonacci sequence is also linked to another mysterious number—approximately 1.618034—known as phi, or the golden ratio. A ratio is a relationship between two numbers. A ratio of 2:1 means the first number is twice as big as the second one. If you divide any number in the Fibonacci sequence by the one before it, you get a number close to phi. Some artists, including Leonardo da Vinci, believed phi had magical qualities and designed their paintings based on the proportions of the golden ratio.

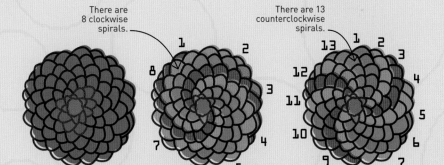

There are 8 clockwise spirals.

There are 13 counterclockwise spirals.

Fibonacci spiral

If you look closely at the florets and seeds in some flower heads, such as sunflowers, or the design of a pine cone, you can see two sets of spirals, turning in opposite directions. The number of spirals is a Fibonacci number, as shown above.

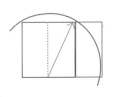

ACTIVITY

Beautiful math

Try your hand at some mathematical art. First draw a golden rectangle from a sequence of squares and then use it to make a golden spiral.

You will need:
- Paper
- Pencils
- Ruler
- Compass

Step 1
Draw a small square and mark a cross on the point halfway along the bottom. Place the point of a compass on the cross, with the pencil end on one of the top corners, and draw a wide curve as shown left.

Step 2
Use a ruler to extend the square to the point where it meets the curve, and draw in the other lines, as shown, to complete the rectangle.

Step 3
Using the new rectangle's longest side as a guide, draw a square below it as shown at left. Using the compass, draw a curve between the corners.

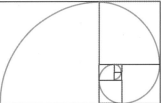

Step 4
Continue drawing larger and larger squares and drawing in the curves and you will soon have a golden spiral.

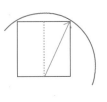

Blaise Pascal

Blaise Pascal (1623–62) was a scientist, inventor, and mathematician. He was also interested in religion, and as a result of his interest in probability (see right). His reasoning will give you a religious man, as a result of his interest was that if God exists, being religious will give you a chance of going to heaven. And if God doesn't exist, it doesn't matter what you believe.

Triangular treasury

Pascal's triangle is easy to construct. You just make each number the sum of the two numbers above. It's no wonder the resulting pyramid is so popular with mathematicians. It contains so many of their favorite number patterns, including triangular and square numbers, powers, and even the Fibonacci sequence.

Each number is the sum of the two above— 6 is 1 plus 5.

You can add as many rows as you like—can you work out the numbers in each row?

Probability

The likelihood something will happen is called probability (see pages 100–101). Here's how Pascal used the triangle to work out the probability that, when tossing five coins, all of them will land heads up.

Step 1

There are six possible outcomes (0, 1, 2, 3, 4, or 5 heads), so look at the sixth row of the triangle:
1, 5, 10, 10, 5, 1.

Step 2

Match the alternatives for each outcome to numbers in the triangle's sixth line:

0 heads = 1
1 head = 5
2 heads = 10
3 heads = 10
4 heads = 5
5 heads = 1

Step 3

Now add the row of numbers:
$1 + 5 + 10 + 10 + 5 + 1 = 32$

Step 4

To find the probability of all five coins being heads, take the number next to 5 heads, which is 1, and compare it to the total of 32. This tells you that the probability of five heads is 1 in 32—if you toss the coins 32 times, they will probably all be heads just once.

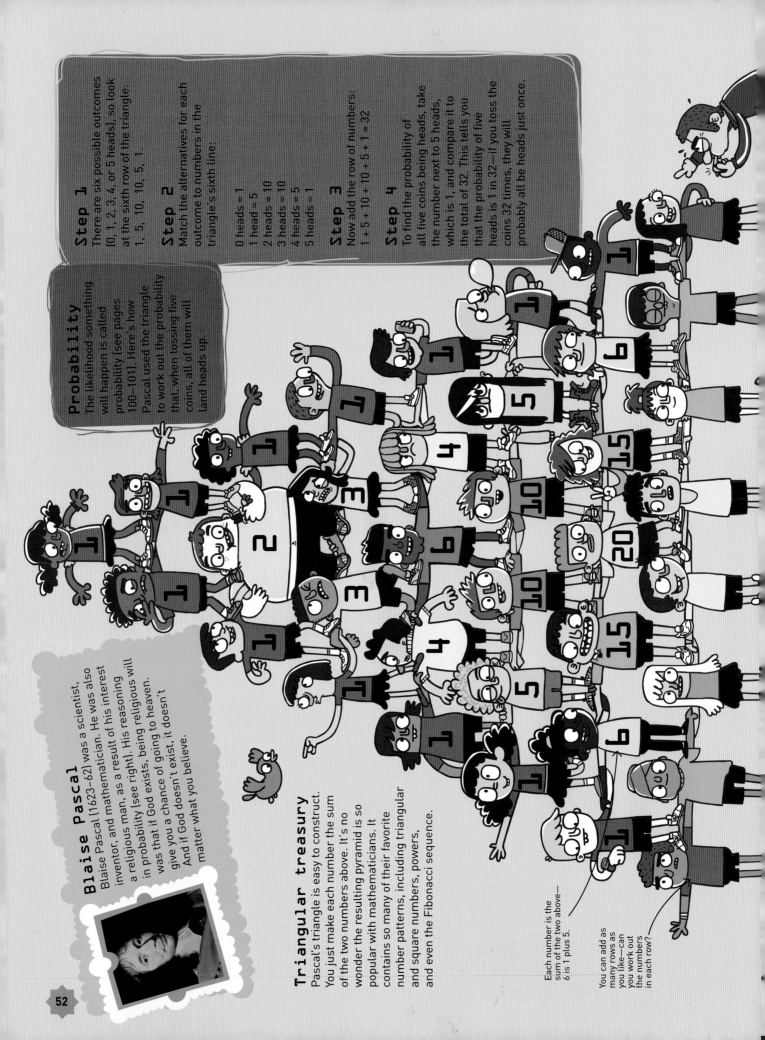

PASCAL'S TRIANGLE

Centuries ago, Indian and Chinese mathematicians discovered the strange properties of a triangular stack of numbers. In the 1600s, the French mathematician Blaise Pascal used the triangle to study the laws of probability. From then on, it was called Pascal's triangle.

Looking for patterns

Pascal's triangle is full of fascinating number patterns. Here are just a few of them.

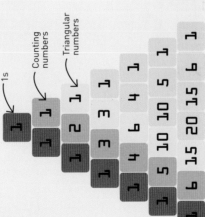

1s
Counting numbers
Triangular numbers

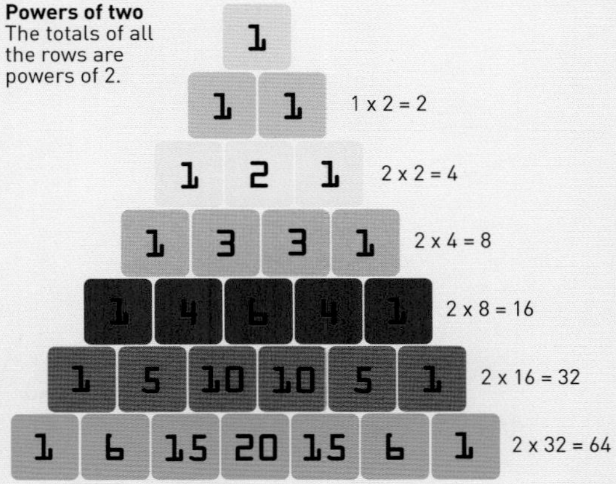

Fibonacci numbers
Adding up the shallow diagonals, shown here in different colors, reveals the Fibonacci sequence.

1
2
3
5
8
13

Powers of two
The totals of all the rows are powers of 2.

$1 \times 2 = 2$
$2 \times 2 = 4$
$2 \times 4 = 8$
$2 \times 8 = 16$
$2 \times 16 = 32$
$2 \times 32 = 64$

Hockey stick sums
Starting from the 1s at the edge, follow a diagonal of numbers. Stop anywhere inside the triangle, turn down in the opposite direction in a "hockey stick" pattern and you'll get their sum.

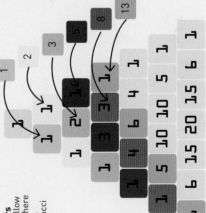

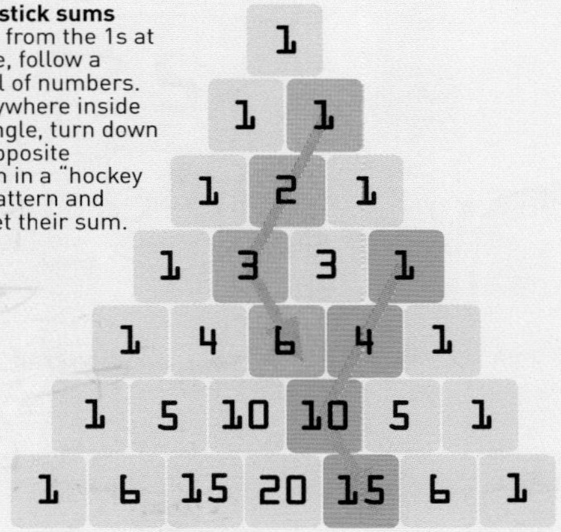

In a way, computers started with Pascal, who built the first well-known mechanical calculating machine in 1645.

ACTIVITY

Braille challenge

Braille is a system of raised dots that blind people can "read" by running their fingers over them. Each letter is a different arrangement of six points, in three rows of two. A point can either be raised up so that it can be felt, or left flat. The first three letters are shown below. The big dots represent raised points and the small ones represent flat points. Can you work out how many possible combinations of this pattern there are?

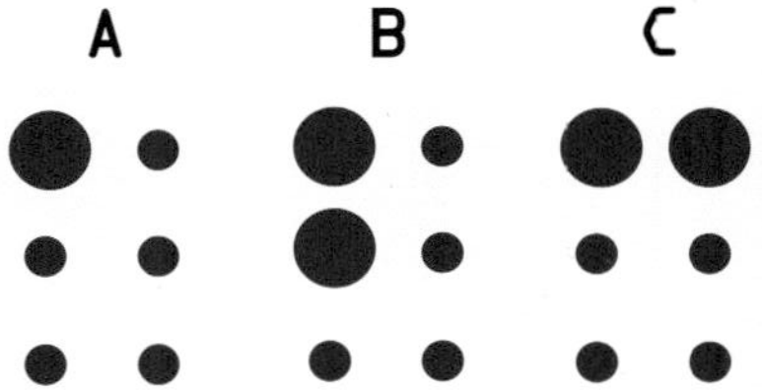

A   B   C

Step 1
As in the example above, work out how many arrangements there are for each number of dots from 0 to 6. For example, with 0 dots there is one arrangement, with 1 dot, there are six possible places the dot could go. Can you spot this pattern in Pascal's triangle?

Step 2
Add the numbers of combinations together. What is your total?

Step 3
Now work out the number of outcomes for a four-point pattern. Which row of the triangle can help you this time?

53

MAGIC SQUARES

One day, more than 4,000 years ago, Emperor Yu of China found a turtle in the Yellow River. Its shell was made up of nine squares, each with a number from 1 to 9 written on it. Stranger still, the sum of any row, column, or diagonal in this 3 x 3 square was 15. It was the world's first magic square.

16	3	2	13
5	10	11	8
9	6	7	12
4	15	14	1

Sensational sums

True or not, Emperor Yu's story introduced the world to the amazing properties of magic squares. In the square on the left, add up the numbers in each row or each column. Now try adding those running diagonally from corner to corner, or those just in the corners, or the four in the center. Have you found the magic number?

Making magic

Can you complete these magic squares? Use each number only once. The magic number is given below each square.

	7	
9		
4		

Easy (number range: 1–9)
Magic number: 15

7		9	
	11		16
	6		
	13	8	1

Medium (number range: 1–16)
Magic number: 34

	18				23
	25		27	22	31
34	9	1	10		21
6		30	28		16
	14	29	8	20	
	15	35	17	13	

Hard (number range: 1–36)
Magic number: 111

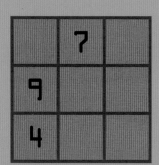

Adaptable square

In this magic square, the numbers in the rows, columns, and diagonals add up to the magic number of 22. However, you can reset the magic number by simply adding to or taking away from the numbers in the white boxes. Try adding 1 to each white box number, for example—the magic number will become 23.

A knight's tour

In the game of chess, a knight can move only in an L shape, as shown below for the moves from 1 to 2 to 3. Follow the full knight's tour around this magic square, visiting each position just once. On an 8 x 8 square, there are 26,534,728,821,064 possible tours that take the knight back to the square on which he began. So take an empty grid and find some more routes yourself.

1	48	31	50	33	16	63	18
30	51	46	3	62	19	14	35
47	2	49	32	15	34	17	64
52	29	4	45	20	61	36	13
5	44	25	56	9	40	21	60
28	53	8	41	24	57	12	37
43	6	55	26	39	10	59	22
54	27	42	7	58	23	38	11

Your own magic square

Make a magic square using knight's-tour moves. Place a 1 anywhere in the bottom row, then move like a knight, in an L, through the other squares to place the numbers 2, 3, 4, and so on, following these rules:

- Move two squares up and one to the right if you can.
- If the square you reach is already full, write your number on the square directly beneath the last number instead.
- Imagine the square wraps around so the top meets the bottom and the two sides meet—if you move off one edge of the square, re-enter on the other side.

So, on this example, from the 3 you move up and right to the second bottom-left square to place a 4. After placing the 5, the L move takes you to the square already occupied by 1, so place the 6 directly below 5 instead. Continue in this way to fill the grid.

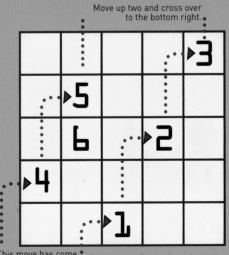

Move up two and cross over to the bottom right.

This move has come from the 3, top right.

This move is 5, but since the square is occupied, the 6 must go beneath the 5.

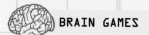
MISSING NUMBERS

Number games such as Sudoku, Sujiko, and Kakuro are great for exercising the brain. These puzzles are all about logical thinking and some arithmetic. To find the numbers you're looking for, you need to use your powers of deduction.

Sudoku

This puzzle consists of a 9 x 9 grid. The numbers 1–9 appear only once in each subgrid, vertical column, and horizontal row. Using the numbers already in the grid, you need to figure out which number should fill an empty box. Each box you fill gives an additional clue to solving the puzzle.

> A good place to look first is the row, column, or subgrid with the most numbers filled in. Check the remaining numbers to find a good starting point.

Completed grid

2	5	7	4	8	1	9	6	3
1	9	3	6	2	7	5	4	8
8	4	6	5	3	9	1	7	2
3	6	1	7	5	8	2	9	4
9	8	5	1	4	2	7	3	6
7	2	4	9	6	3	8	5	1
6	3	2	8	7	5	4	1	9
4	7	9	2	1	6	3	8	5
5	1	8	3	9	4	6	2	7

Column

Row

Subgrid

> Never just guess where a number goes. If there are a number of possibilities, write them small in pencil in the corner until you're sure.

Starter

1		6	4	8			3	
	8			2	3			6
	2						9	7
		2	8		7			
	1			3			7	
		7	9		2	4	8	
9	4			6			1	2
7	3						5	
	6	8		7	5	9	3	

> Look for sets of three numbers, or "triplets." The number 7 appears in the bottom and middle subgrids of the middle block above, which means that the third 7 must go in the left-hand column of the top box. Check the rows and you'll see there's only one place it can go.

Slightly harder

7		5			3	1	2	
9	6		5		1			
2				4				
					9	2		
8		9				5		3
		7	3					
			6					2
	1		2			6	5	
3	2	4			9		8	

Sujiko

In a Sujiko puzzle, the number in each circle is the sum of the numbers in the four surrounding squares. Using the numbers 1-9 only once, work out the arrangement of numbers needed to fill in the blank squares.

Here's how

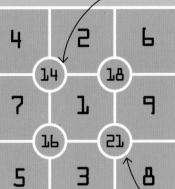

4 + 2 + 7 + 1 = 14

1 + 9 + 3 + 8 = 21

Over to you...

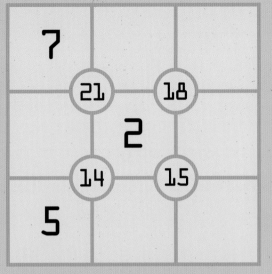

👁 You must do this using the numbers 1–9 only once. We've completed one here to show you how it works. Now try to fill in the grid above yourself.

Look at the number 14 in the bottom left circle. To reach a total of 14, the sum of the empty squares must also total 7, so which other combinations are there?

Kakuro

A Kakuro puzzle is a little like a crossword puzzle, except with numbers. Fill in the blank squares with the numbers 1–9. They can appear more than once. The numbers must add up to the total shown either above the column or to the side of the row.

What to do

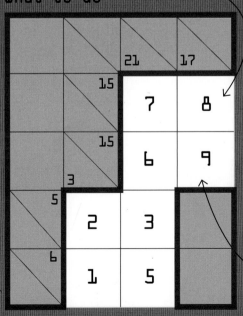

The numbers in this column add up to 17

The numbers in this row add up to 15

Now try this

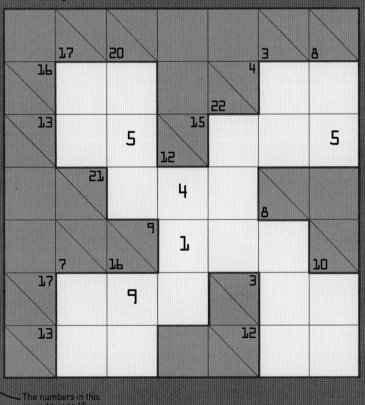

Karl Gauss

Many people consider Gauss to be the greatest mathematician ever. He made breakthroughs in many areas of math, including statistics, algebra, and number theory, and he used his skills to make many discoveries in physics. Gauss was also exceptionally good at mental arithmetic, even at a young age.

Gauss was born in this house in Brunswick, Germany. His parents were very poor, so his education was paid for by the Duke of Brunswick.

Early life
Gauss was born in 1777, the only child of poor, uneducated parents. From an early age, it was clear that Gauss was a child prodigy with an extraordinary talent for mathematics. When he was just three years old, he spotted a mistake in his father's accounts. Later, Gauss amazed his teacher at school by coming up with his own way to add a long series of numbers.

Proving the impossible
Gauss was gifted at both math and languages, and when he was 19, he had to decide which to study. He settled on math after completing the supposedly impossible mathematical task of drawing a regular 17-sided shape (a heptadecagon) using only a ruler and a compass. His discovery led to a new branch of math.

A page of Gauss's mathematical notes from a letter he wrote in July 1800 to Johann Hellwig, math professor at Brunswick's military academy.

Gauss wanted his greatest discovery, the 17-sided heptadecagon, carved on his tombstone, but the stonemason refused, telling him it would look just like a circle.

Sun

Ceres

The lost planet
In 1801, the dwarf planet Ceres was discovered, but astronomers lost track of it after it passed behind the Sun. Gauss used his math skills to locate Ceres. From the few observations that had been made before it disappeared, Gauss was able to predict where it would appear next. He was right!

Mars

Jupiter

Science from math

Gauss was fascinated by math and also by its practical uses in science. This led him to play a part in inventing the electric telegraph—a major means of communication in the days before telephones and radios. Gauss also studied Earth's magnetism and invented a device for measuring magnetic fields. In recognition of this, a unit of magnetism is named after him.

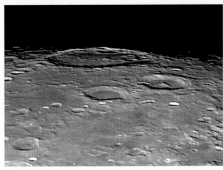

Many of the moon's craters are named after famous scientists. The Gauss crater sits on the northeastern edge of the moon's near side.

Correspondence with Sophie Germain

Gauss often communicated with French mathematician Sophie Germain about topics such as number theory. Unable to study or teach at the college level because she was a woman, Germain initially used a male pseudonym to write to Gauss and other esteemed mathematicians. Gauss campaigned for her to be awarded an honorary degree in recognition of her achievements, but the French Academy refused.

Cool curve

When a set of information, such as the heights of a group of people, is plotted on a bar graph (see page 102), it commonly takes the shape of a particular curve. At either end of the graph are the shortest and tallest people, with most people in the middle. Gauss was the first to identify this curve, calling it a bell curve. It can be used to analyze data, design experiments, work out errors, and make predictions.

This German 10-euro note featured a portrait of Gauss and a bell curve.

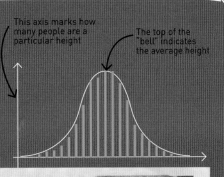

This axis marks how many people are a particular height

The top of the "bell" indicates the average height

All sorts of things have been named in Gauss's honor, including this German ship sent to explore Antarctica in 1901. During the expedition, the crew discovered an extinct volcano, which they named Gaussberg.

INFINITY

Almost everyone finds it difficult to grasp the meaning of infinity. It's like an endless corridor that goes on forever without any end or limits. But infinity is a useful idea in mathematics. Many sequences and series go on to infinity and so do the numbers you count with. It's like saying that there's no largest number, because whatever number you think of, you can always add another.

The infinity symbol was invented in 1655. It refers to something that has no beginning or end.

Is infinity real?
Just because infinity is useful in math, it doesn't mean that infinite things definitely exist. For example, it's possible that the Universe is infinite and contains an infinite number of stars. Time, too, will probably go on without ever ending. This is called eternity.

Anything is possible
Given a long enough time, anything can happen. For example, a roomful of monkeys tapping on keyboards would eventually type out the complete works of Shakespeare. This is because the works of Shakespeare are finite (have an end), and given infinite time, eventually all possible finite sequences of letters will appear.

Properties of infinity
Although infinity is not really a number, it can be thought of as the limit, or end, of a series of numbers. Therefore, it can be used in equations:

$$\infty + 1 = \infty$$

$$\infty + \infty = \infty$$

$$\infty \times \infty = \infty$$

$$\infty - 1{,}000{,}000{,}000 = \infty$$

Try exploring the math of infinity on a calculator. Divide 1 by larger and larger numbers and see what happens. What do you think you would get if you could divide by an infinitely large number?

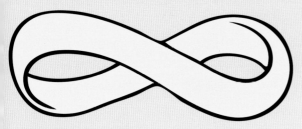

Infinite math
The infinity symbol looks like an 8 on its side. However, the infinity symbol isn't used to represent the idea of infinity in sequences. Instead, infinite sequences of numbers are written with three dots at the end. For example, the numbers you count with are 1, 2, 3, ... Other sequences might have no beginning and no end. For example: ...-2, -1, 0, 1, 2, ...

Exploring infinity
It is not just mathematicians that have explored the idea of infinity, but philosophers, writers, and artists, too. Dutch artist M.C. Escher (1898–1972) is one of several creators who have used the idea of infinity, often including interlocking repeated images in his graphics. There is even a variation of chess called infinite chess, in which the chessboard can go on endlessly!

Endless space
Most people don't like the idea that the Universe might be infinite and go on forever, and that there is no farthest star. If that were the case, then there would be an infinite number of Earths and an infinite number of "you's" too. It's difficult to imagine, but this idea goes some way toward explaining why some scientists assume that the Universe must have an outer limit.

Going on forever
Infinity is impossible to fully understand or imagine. You can get a sense of it, though, by standing between two mirrors. Since each mirror reflects the other mirror, you'll get to see images of yourself stretching endlessly away!

Georg Cantor
The first person to grapple with the math of infinity was Georg Cantor (1845–1918), who believed in different kinds of infinity. Mathematicians hated his ideas, which upset traditional ways of thinking, and he faced great hostility. Today, his theories are accepted and have changed math forever.

NUMBERS WITH MEANING

All over the world, people have lucky, and sometimes unlucky, numbers. But why is this? The reasons range from religious significance to the sound or look of the number.

17

In Italy, the number 17 is very unlucky. Italian planes often don't have a row 17 because superstitious airlines leave it out. The reason is that it's written XVII in Roman numerals. This may look harmless, but jumble up the letters and you get VIXI, which means "my life is over!"

4

In China, Japan, and Korea, the word for four sounds like "death." In Hong Kong (China), some tall buildings leave out floor numbers with four in them, such as floors 4, 14, 24, 34, and 40. So a building with a 50th floor at the top does not always have 50 floors!

666

This number is very unlucky in Christian culture because it is recorded in the Bible as the number of the beast, or the devil. In China, however, the word for six sounds like "smooth" or "flowing," so saying six three times in a row is like saying "everything is running smoothly."

14

In China, the number to avoid is 14 because it sounds like "want to die." In South America, however, 14 is considered very lucky because it's twice the lucky number 7... so you can double your luck.

5

In the Islamic faith, five is a sacred number. There are five major parts to the faith, called the Pillars of Islam. Followers of Islam pray five times a day, and there are five types of Islamic law and five law-giving prophets.

42

Do not shout out the number 42 in Japan! When the numbers four and two are pronounced together in Japanese, they sound like "going to death."

7

Seven is generally considered a lucky or even magic number. In Irish folklore, a seventh son of a seventh son is supposed to have magic powers. Iranian cats supposedly have seven, not nine, lives. And in the Jewish and Christian faiths, the number seven symbolizes perfection.

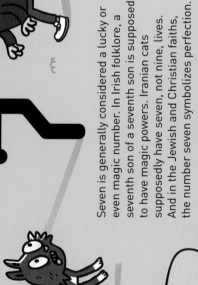

13

Some people prefer to stay inside on Friday the 13th, because 13 is such an unlucky number. For Christians, it is linked to the 13th apostle, Judas, who betrayed Jesus. However, it's not all bad. Jews and Sikhs think 13 is a very lucky number.

3

If you want to impress someone in Russia, do everything three times. The number is considered very lucky because it represents the Holy Christian Trinity—God the Father, the Son, and the Holy Spirit. So remember to kiss people three times when you meet, and bring three flowers for someone really special.

8 8 8 8

In China, the number eight symbolizes prosperity and wealth, so three eights in a row means that success and money are tripled! License plates, houses, and telephone numbers that feature this super-lucky number sell for vast amounts.

60

The Ancient Babylonians loved 60 and used it as a base for all their mathematical calculations. We don't count like them anymore, but some elements of their number system survive, such as the 60 minutes in an hour and 60 seconds in a minute.

40

In Russia, a quick way to be forgiven for your sins is to kill a spider! One dead spider wipes out 40 sins. The number 40 also occurs frequently in Christianity and often refers to periods of reflection or punishment. The prophet Moses spent 40 days and 40 nights on Mount Sinai and Jesus fasted in the wilderness for 40 days.

Counting on numbers

It's easy to understand why a number that sounds like "going to death" makes people feel uneasy, but why do we give other numbers meanings? It's probably because a long time ago, before we understood science, people felt a need to understand and explain why bad or good things happened to them. If there was no other likely explanation, people looked for a pattern in the numbers and blamed that for their problems, such as disease or a spell of bad weather. Similarly, having "lucky" numbers gave people some hope that things might get better!

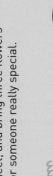

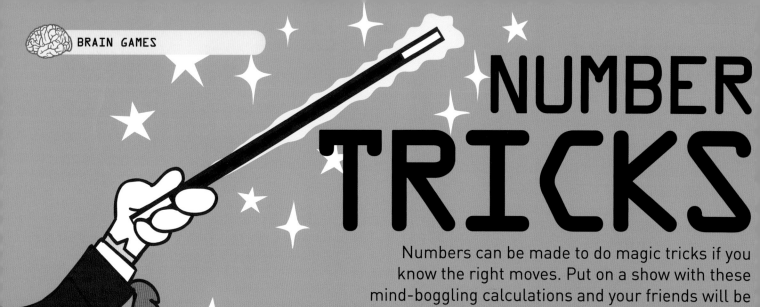

NUMBER TRICKS

Numbers can be made to do magic tricks if you know the right moves. Put on a show with these mind-boggling calculations and your friends will be convinced you're either a magician or a genius.

Guess a birthday

Let the math do all the work for you with this trick to reveal a friend's date of birth.

Step 1

Hand your friend a calculator and ask her to do the following:

- Add 18 to her birth month
- Multiply the answer by 25
- Subtract 333
- Multiply the answer by 8
- Subtract 554
- Divide the answer by 2
- Add her birth date day
- Multiply the answer by 5
- Add 692
- Multiply the answer by 20
- Add only the last two digits of her birth year

Step 2

Build up suspense and then ask her to subtract 32940. The answer will be her birthday!

Pocket change

Convince a friend of your extraordinary mathematical powers by correctly guessing the amount of change he has in his pockets.

Step 1

Find a friend with some loose change in his pockets. Ask him to add up the coins, but you don't want a total of more than $1. If he's got too much, ask him to remove some coins. Then ask him to do the following:

- Take his age and multiply it by 2
- Add 5
- Multiply this sum by 50
- Subtract 365
- Add the amount of the loose change from his pockets
- Add 115 to get the final answer

Step 2

Amaze your friend by revealing that the first two digits of the number are his age, and the last two digits are the amount of change from his pocket.

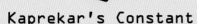

Kaprekar's Constant

Tell a friend that, by following one simple magic formula, you can turn any four-digit number into 6174 in seven steps or fewer.

Step 1
Get your friend to write down any four-digit number that has at least two different numbers, so 1744 is fine, but 5555 is not.

Step 2
Tell her to put the digits in ascending and descending order. So, 1744 would give 1447 and 7441. Instruct her to subtract the small number from the large number. If the answer isn't 6174, repeat the last two steps using the answer of the first calculation. Within seven tries, she will end up with 6174.

This curious number pattern was discovered by the Indian mathematician D.R. Kaprekar.

Predicting the answer

This trick reveals your ability to predict the right answer. In fact, you are just disguising some simple math.

Step 1
Before you begin this trick, take the current year and double it—for example, 2012 x 2 = 4024. Write the answer on a piece of paper and fold it to hide the number.

Step 2
Find a volunteer, hand him the folded piece of paper, and ask him to do the following:
• Think of a significant historical date, and add his age to it—for example, 1969 + 13 = 1982.
• Next, add the year of his birth to the number of years that have passed since that historical date—for example, 1999 + 43 = 2042.
• Combine the two answers, so 1982 + 2042 = 4024.

Step 3
Ask your friend to open the piece of paper and enjoy the amazed look on his face.

Find somebody's age

You can also use a series of calculations to reveal the age of someone older than nine.

Step 1
Make sure your victim doesn't mind you revealing his age, then give him a piece of paper and ask him to do the following:
• Multiply the first number of his age by 5, then add 3.
• Double this figure, and add the second digit of his age.

Step 2
Get him to write the total down and show it to you. Pretend to be doing complex calculations, but simply subtract 6 and you should have his age.

PUZZLING PRIMES

Of all of the numbers that exist, primes are the ones that mathematicians love most. That's because prime numbers have special properties. A prime is a number that can be divided into whole numbers only by itself and the number 1. So 4 is not a prime, because it can be divided by 2. However, 3 is a prime because no numbers can be divided into it except for itself and 1.

The search continues

There is no known method for discovering primes. Each new one is more difficult to find than the last. It's not often that math makes the headlines, but when a new prime number is found, it's big news. In 1991, the tiny country of Liechtenstein even issued a stamp to mark the discovery of a new prime number.

Prime pyramid
All of the numbers in this number pyramid are primes. The next number in the pattern would be 333,333,331, but surprisingly it isn't a prime—it can be divided by 17 to give 19,607,843.

```
      31
     331
    3331
   33331
  333331
 3333331
33333331
```

ACTIVITY

Sifting for primes

Large prime numbers can be found only by computers. However, in about 300 BCE, the Greek mathematician Eratosthenes discovered how to find small ones by using this "sieve" system.

👁 Draw a 10 x 10 grid and fill it with the numbers 1 to 100. Cross out the number 1, which is not classified as a prime number.

👁 The next number is 2. There is no number except 1 that can divide into it, so it is a prime. Circle it.

👁 Any number that can be produced by multiplying by 2 cannot be a prime. So, except for the number 2 itself, cross out all the multiples of 2.

👁 The next number is 3. There is no number except 1 that can divide into it, so it's a prime. Circle it. Again, any number that can be produced by multiplying by 3 cannot be a prime, so cross out all the numbers that are multiples of 3, except for the number 3 itself.

👁 You should have already crossed out all the multiples of 4 when you crossed out the multiples of 2. Now cross out all multiples of 5 and 7 (again, except for themselves).

👁 All of the remaining numbers are primes.

1	2	3	4	5	6	7	8	9	10
11	12	13	14	15	16	17	18	19	20
21	22	23	24	25	26	27	28	29	30
31	32	33	34	35	36	37	38	39	40
41	42	43	44	45	46	47	48	49	50
51	52	53	54	55	56	57	58	59	60
61	62	63	64	65	66	67	68	69	70
71	72	73	74	75	76	77	78	79	80
81	82	83	84	85	86	87	88	89	90
91	92	93	94	95	96	97	98	99	100

Find the factors

Prime numbers are the building blocks from which other numbers can be made. For instance, 6 can be made by multiplying 2 and 3, so 2 and 3 are called the "prime factors" of 6. Can you find the answers to these prime factor puzzles?

Step 1

There is a number between 30 and 40 with prime factors between 4 and 10. What is the number and its prime factors? To answer this, start by finding the prime numbers between 4 and 10. Now multiply these numbers together to find their products (the answer when two numbers are multiplied together). You'll find there is only one product between 30 and 40.

Step 2

Now find a number between 40 and 60 that has prime factors between 4 and 12. What are its factors?

Crafty cicadas

Prime numbers are even used in nature, in particular by an insect called a cicada. Some species of cicadas live underground as larvae for 13 or 17 years, after which time they emerge as adults to mate. Both 13 and 17 are prime numbers, which means the cicadas are more likely to avoid predators with life cycles of two, three, four, or five years, and therefore stand a better chance of living to see another day.

Prime cube

Write the numbers 1–9 into the squares of a 3 x 3 grid so that each row and column adds up to a prime number. It does not have to be the same prime number each time. We have given you some numbers to start you off, but there are 16 different solutions. How many can you find?

Prime busting

Multiplying two big prime numbers together is relatively easy with the help of a good computer. The result is called a semiprime. But start with a semiprime and try to work backward to find its prime factors, and you're in trouble! It's an almost impossible task. For this reason, primes are used to change messages into nearly unbreakable codes—a process called encryption—to protect banking details and the privacy of e-mails.

In 2009, an international computer project called the Great Internet Mersenne Prime Search (GIMPS) won a $100,000 prize for finding a 12-million-digit prime number.

Shapes and Space

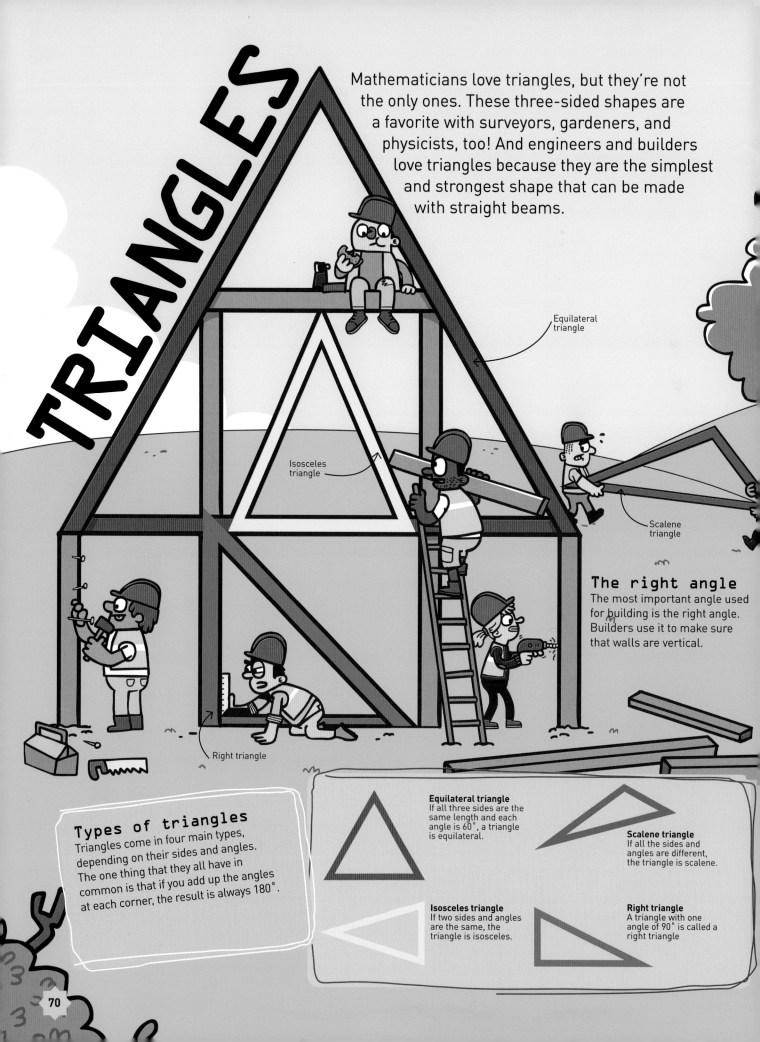

TRIANGLES

Mathematicians love triangles, but they're not the only ones. These three-sided shapes are a favorite with surveyors, gardeners, and physicists, too! And engineers and builders love triangles because they are the simplest and strongest shape that can be made with straight beams.

Equilateral triangle

Isosceles triangle

Scalene triangle

The right angle
The most important angle used for building is the right angle. Builders use it to make sure that walls are vertical.

Right triangle

Types of triangles
Triangles come in four main types, depending on their sides and angles. The one thing that they all have in common is that if you add up the angles at each corner, the result is always 180°.

Equilateral triangle
If all three sides are the same length and each angle is 60°, a triangle is equilateral.

Scalene triangle
If all the sides and angles are different, the triangle is scalene.

Isosceles triangle
If two sides and angles are the same, the triangle is isosceles.

Right triangle
A triangle with one angle of 90° is called a right triangle

The 3-D graphics used in films and computer games are created using triangles.

Super-strong!

If you make a square from four rods, it can easily be forced into a diamond shape. The same is true of pentagons and hexagons—they are easily pushed or pulled out of shape. A triangle of rods, on the other hand, cannot be forced into a different shape without breaking the rods or the joints. This strength is one reason why you'll find triangles used in buildings and bridges.

Measuring areas

You can use triangles to measure the area of any shape that has straight lines. Here's how to do it:

Step 1

Split the area of this shape into right triangles. We have marked the dimensions you need to know.

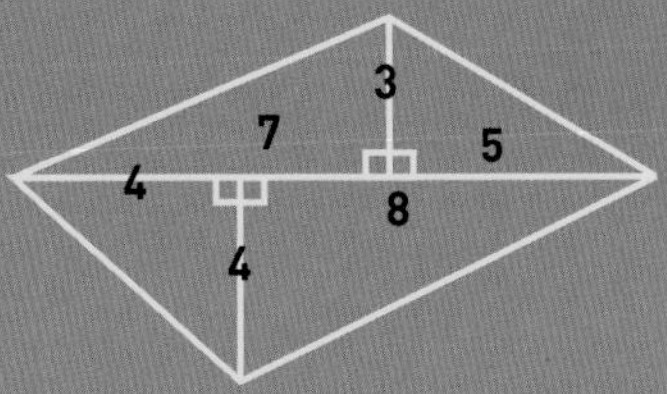

3
7   5
4   8
4

Step 2

A right triangle is simply half a rectangle. So work out the area of each shape as a rectangle, then halve it. So:

$3 \times 7 = 21$
$21 \div 2 = 10.5$

3

7

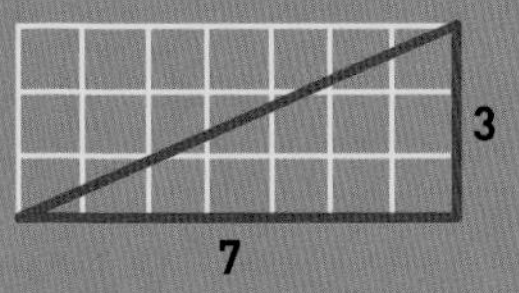

Step 3

Repeat this process for the other triangles, and add them together to get the total area.

Trees and triangles

You can use a right-angled triangle to figure out the height of a tree without climbing it. Work out where you need to place a stick on the ground that would point directly at the top of the tree at an angle of 45°. The distance along the ground between the stick and the tree will then be the same as the height of the tree. If the angle between the stick and the ground is greater than 45°, then the tree would squash you if it fell.

Hipparchus

The Ancient Greek astronomer and mathematician Hipparchus (c. 190–120 BCE) used triangles to help him figure out the measurements of many objects. He didn't stick to just earthly objects, though—he used triangles to work out the distance and size of the Sun and the Moon!

SHAPING UP

The study of shapes is one of the most ancient areas of math. The Ancient Egyptians learned enough about them to build pyramids, measure land, and study the stars. But it was the Ancient Greeks who really came to grips with shapes and discovered many of the ideas and rules that we learn about today.

All four sides

Any shape with four straight sides is called a quadrilateral, and there are connections between them. For example, a square is a type of rectangle, and a rectangle is a type of parallelogram.

Square
When all sides are equal and all corners are right angles, it's a square.

Trapezium
A quadrilateral with one pair of parallel sides of different lengths.

Rectangle
A shape with four right angles and two pairs of opposite sides of equal length.

Kite
This shape has two pairs of adjacent sides of equal length. Opposite sides are not equal.

Rhombus
If all sides are equal, but there are no right angles it's a rhombus.

Parallelogram
A shape that has opposite sides equal in length and parallel to each other.

The math of shapes is called geometry, from the Ancient Greek words for "Earth measuring."

More and more sides

Shapes with five or more sides and angles all have names ending in "-gon." The first part of the name comes from the Greek word for the number of sides. Polygon means "many sides."

Pentagon
5 sides

Hexagon
6 sides

Heptagon
7 sides

Octagon
8 sides

Nonagon
9 sides

Decagon
10 sides

Dodecagon
12 sides

Even more sides

The more sides a polygon has, the closer it becomes to a circle.

13—tridecagon
14—tetradecagon
15—pentadecagon
16—hexadecagon
17—heptadecagon
18—octadecagon
19—enneadecagon
20—icosagon
100—hectogon
1000—chiliagon
10,000—myriagon
1,000,000—megagon

Seeing symmetry

Many shapes have a quality called symmetry. There are two types—lateral and rotational. If a shape can be folded so that both halves are identical, it has lateral symmetry. If a shape looks the same when you turn it part-way around a central point, it has rotational symmetry. This shapely quality is important in both math and science.

Lateral line
The line down the middle of a symmetrical shape is called the axis of symmetry. A butterfly has one axis of symmetry.

Turning point
If you turn the book upside down, you'll see that this swirl has rotational symmetry, because it looks exactly the same the other way up.

Snowflakes are made of hexagon-shaped crystals, which is why they all have six arms.

Animals with an odd number of limbs are rare, but a starfish has five. As a result, it has five axes of lateral symmetry, as well as rotational symmetry.

The perfect pattern of spider webs is the most efficient way to build a large trap as quickly as possible.

Shapes in nature

Regular shapes and symmetry can be found in the natural world. Most animals have an axis of symmetry, and most plants have rotational symmetry. These shapes are partly due to the way living things grow, but can also be useful for the way they live.

Tiny sea creatures, called diatoms, are found in a wide variety of shapes, with either rotational or lateral symmetry.

Bees build honeycombs using hexagonal cells because this shape uses the least wax.

Flatfish are born symmetrical, but as they develop both eyes move over to the same side of their head and they become asymmetrical.

A perfect fit

When shapes fit together like tiles, without any gaps, the pattern is called tessellation. Triangles, identical quadrilaterals, and hexagons tessellate, but pentagons do not. Some mixtures of shapes tessellate, like octagons and squares.

Symmetrical you

Humans look symmetrical—it's a sensible way to organize the parts of our bodies. But are we?

The features of your face are slightly different on each side. Hold a mirror along your nose and look into another mirror and you will see.

Inside your body, the heart is more on the left and the liver is more on the right.

Most people have one foot that's a little bigger than the other, and one dominant hand.

If you tried to walk in a straight line in a thick fog, so you could see nothing to keep you on course, you would in fact veer slightly to one side and walk in a big circle. The asymmetrical nature of your body pulls you slightly to one side.

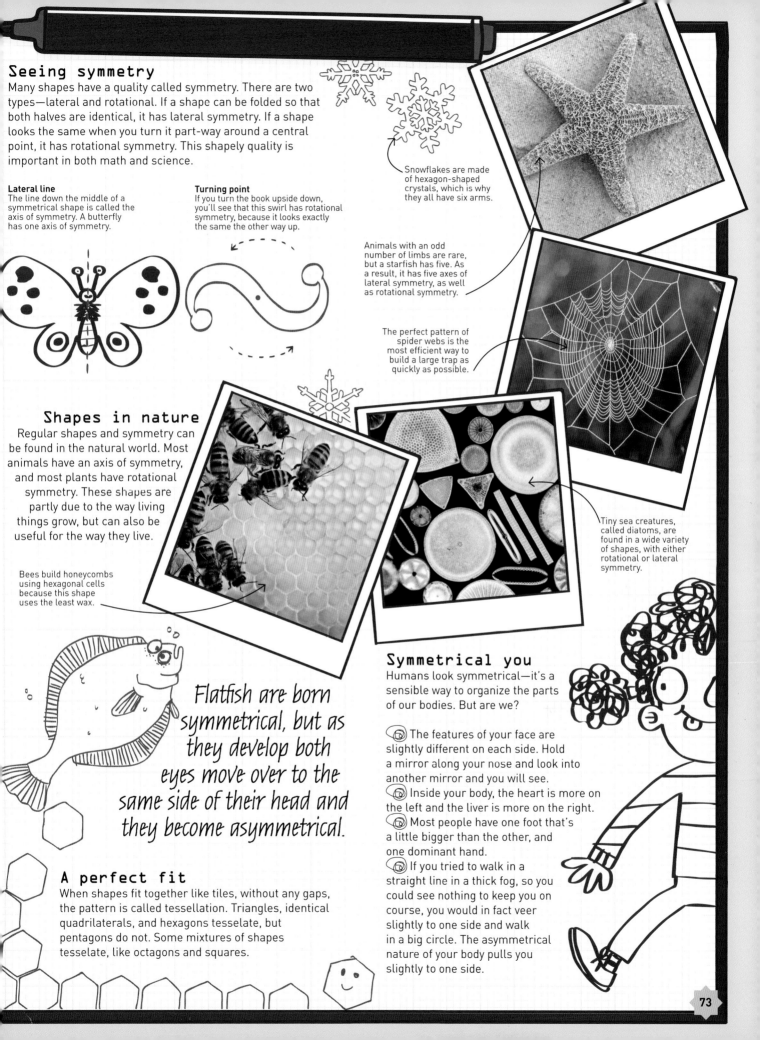

SHAPE SHIFTING

The puzzles on these pages are designed to exercise your brain's sense of 2-D shapes. There are shapes within shapes to find, and others to cut up and create. You'll have square eyes by the end!

Triangle tally

Take a good look at this pyramid of triangles, and what do you see? Lots of triangles, that's for sure, but do you know how many? You will need to concentrate hard to count all the triangles within triangles—things are not always as simple as they appear!

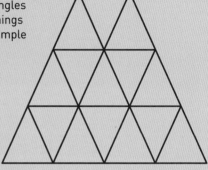

Tantalizing tangrams

You can use small shapes to make an endless variety of others. In China, people used this fact to create the game of tangrams. Using just seven shapes, you can make hundreds of different designs.

You will need:
• Square piece of paper
• Scissors
• Colored pens or pencils

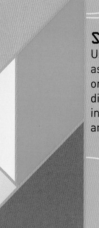

Step 1

Using the tangram at left as a guide, draw a square on a piece of paper and divide it into seven individual shapes. Color and cut out each shape.

Step 2

Practice making pictures by rearranging the colored pieces to create this rabbit.

Step 3

Now try making these images. We haven't shown you the different colors of the pieces to make things trickier. Then have fun creating your own designs.

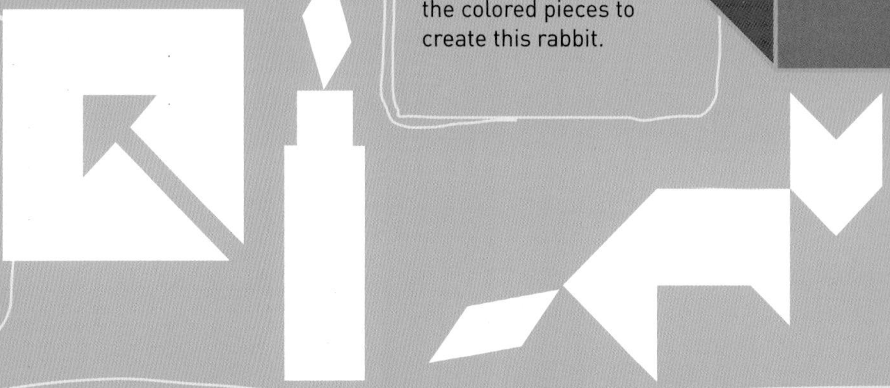

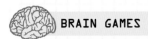

Shapes within shapes

These shapes can be split into equal pieces. To give you a head start, the first shapes are divided already.

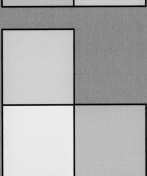

Square thinking

This square has been divided into four, but how would you divide it into five identical pieces? You need to think laterally.

Dividing the L

This L shape has also been cut up into three identical pieces, but can you divide it into four identical shapes? The clue is in the shape itself. How about about six identical pieces?

Boxed in

These matchstick puzzles are a great way to exercise your lateral thinking. If you don't have matchsticks, use toothpicks instead.

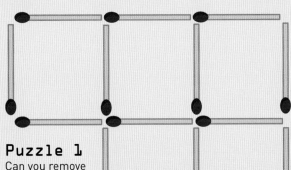

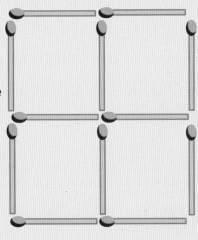

Puzzle 1

Can you remove three matches to leave just three squares?

Puzzle 2

Lay out 12 matches as shown. Can you move just two matches to make seven squares?

Dare to be square

The challenge here is to draw the grids below not using a series of lines, but using squares—and the least number possible. The good news is that the first one has been done for you. The bad news is that they get trickier and trickier.

Here's how

You can draw this 2 x 2 grid using just 3 squares, shown here in red.

Go it alone

Now try drawing this 3 x 3 grid using just 4 squares.

4 x 4 challenge

What is the fewest number of squares needed for this grid?

Look around you and you'll see circles everywhere—coins, wheels, even your dinner plate! A circle is a great shape and looks so simple, but try to draw one and you'll discover it has curious qualities.

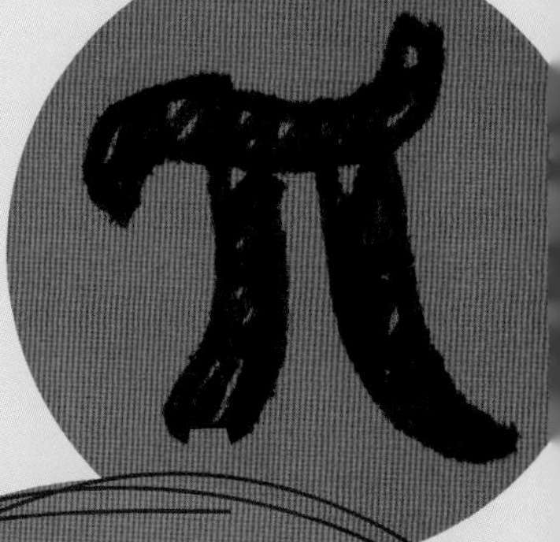

ROUND AND ROUND

circumference

diameter

radius

In circles

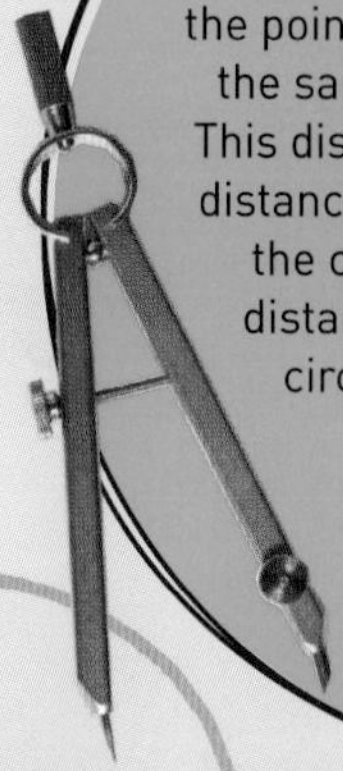

A circle is a shape where all the points around the edge are exactly the same distance from the center. This distance is called the radius. The distance across a whole circle through the center is the diameter, and the distance around a circle is called the circumference. One simple way to draw a circle is by using a pair of compasses.

What is pi?

In any circle—whether it's a bicycle wheel or a clock face—the circumference divided by the diameter equals 3.141392... This special number is called pi and was even given its own symbol—π—by the Ancient Greeks. It goes on forever. The distances in a circle are related to pi. For example, the circumference is π multiplied by the diameter.

3.141592653589...

ACTIVITY

Circle to hexagon

Draw a circle with a compass and then see if you can follow the pattern below and turn it into a hexagon. We've provided some tips to help you.

Start by placing the sharp point of the compasses somewhere on the edge of the circle.

Swing the compasses to draw a curve that goes through the circle's centre and crosses its edge at two points. Place the sharp point of the compass on a point and repeat until you have the pattern shown here.

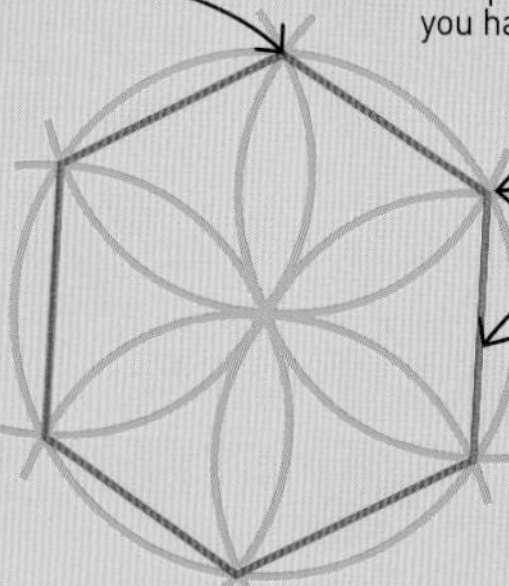

Join the points using a ruler to create a hexagon.

In 2011, Japanese mathematician Shigero Kondo took 371 days to work out pi to 10 trillion decimal places.

Not quite a circle

Many people think planets orbit the Sun in circles, but in fact their paths are ellipses. An ellipse, or oval, looks like a squashed circle, but is still a very precise shape. A circle has one central point, but an ellipsis has two key points, called foci. You can see this if you try drawing one (see right).

(see right)

Draw an ellipse

Here's how to draw an ellipse using two pins and some string. Try using different lengths of string and see what happens.

Step 1

Press two pins into a piece of paper on a board. These are the two foci of the ellipse.

Step 2

Make a circle of string that will fit loosely around the pins, and loop it around them. Place the pencil inside the loop and pull it tight to draw a curve around the two foci.

On a curve

A parabola is a special type of curve that is common in nature and useful in technology and engineering. If you throw a ball, it falls to the ground in a curve roughly the shape of a parabola. You can also see parabolas. in man-made structures, such as the dishes of radio telescopes and satellites. The gently curved sides of the dishes gather signals and reflect them to focus on a central antenna.

Find the center of a circle with a book

Books are handy for doing math in more ways than one. Draw a circle and find a book that's larger than the circle. Then follow these steps for a fun way to find the circle's center.

Step 1

Place a corner of the book on the edge of the circle (A) and mark where the two edges cross the circle (see two points, B).

Step 2

Remove the book and draw a line between the two points. This is a diameter of the circle.

Step 3

Repeat steps 1 and 2 to find a second diameter (see two points, C). The point where the two diameters cross is the center of the circle.

THE THIRD DIMENSION

The three dimensions of space are length, width, and height, and describing 3-D shapes is an important area of math. Every object has its shape for a reason, so understanding shapes helps us understand natural objects, and also design artificial ones.

Building shapes

Some regular 3-D shapes, such as pyramids, can be made by putting 2-D shapes together. In other cases, 3-D shapes like bricks are used to build 3-D shapes like houses. Understanding the math involved helps manufacturers or builders figure out the best way to create their designs.

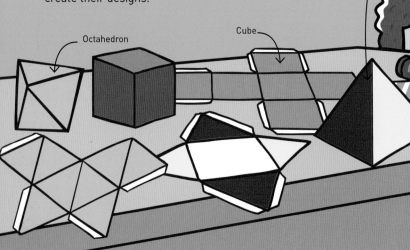

Octahedron

Pyramid

Cube

Tetrahedron

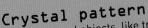
Crystal pattern
Many natural objects, like trees and people, have irregular shapes, but some are very regular—such as crystals. Crystals are made of tiny particles, which join together to make simple shapes, like cubes. As more particles join onto the cubes, they slowly grow bigger and bigger.

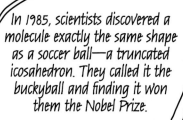
In 1985, scientists discovered a molecule exactly the same shape as a soccer ball—a truncated icosahedron. They called it the buckyball and finding it won them the Nobel Prize.

Spherical world

The simplest 3-D shape is a sphere. It is the shape that contains the most space within the smallest surface. It is also very strong because it has no corners. Objects such as the Sun, planets, and moons are spherical because, as they were forming, gravity pulled their material together.

A dome is a half sphere (hemisphere).

The Earth is a whole set of spherical shells: an inner core, outer core, mantle, and crust.

Most soccer balls are made up of 12 pentagons and 20 hexagons, a shape called a truncated icosahedron.

Stacking and packing

Thinking about 3-D shapes is an important part of design. Packaging, for example, needs to keep to a minimum the weight, cost, and the amount of material used (and usually thrown away). But packaging also needs to protect what's inside, and stack on shelves. A spherical can, for example, would use the least metal, but would be difficult to make, stack, and open up, so cylinders are a better shape.

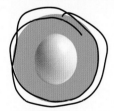

Oval egg

Pear-shaped egg

Perfectly egg-shaped

Eggs are approximately spherical, so they are easy for birds to lay and sit on. This shape also uses less shell than a cube-shaped egg would. But there are a great variety of egg shapes, depending on where the bird nests. Birds that nest in trees, where they are safe, lay very round eggs. Birds that nest on cliff ledges have extra-pointy eggs that roll in circles if they are knocked, rather than off the edge.

Seeing in 3-D

We have two eyes because one is not enough to see in 3-D. Try closing one eye, and then the other, and see how the two pictures are slightly different. The brain takes the two 2-D pictures and, with the help of other clues such as shadows, puts them together to create a 3-D image.

Constructing cubes

To solve this puzzle, you need to picture the pieces in your head, and then rotate them to find the pairs that fit together to make a cube. But there are nine pieces, so there's one shape too many. What are the pairs and which is the shape that will be left over?

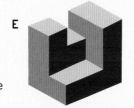
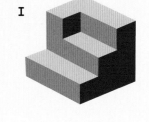
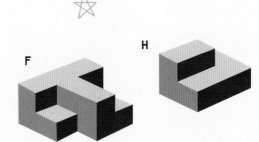
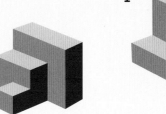
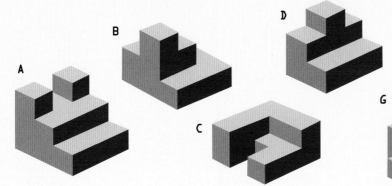
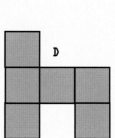
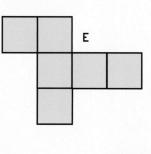

3-D SHAPE PUZZLES

Getting your head around these 3-D shapes is a great workout for the brain, especially since you are looking at them in 2-D. How much easier would it be if you could hold them in your hands to fit them together or fold them!

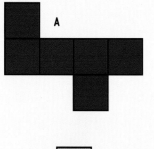

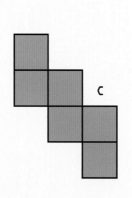

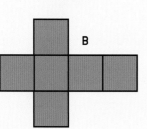

Boxing up

The net of a 3-D shape is what it would look like if it was opened up flat. These are the nets of six cubes—or are they? In fact, one net is wrong and will not fold up to make a cube. Can you figure out which one it is?

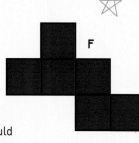

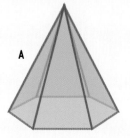
A

Hexagonal pyramid

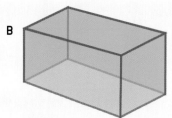
B

Rectangular prism

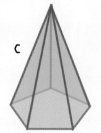
C

Pentagonal pyramid

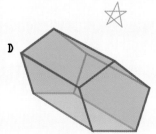
D

Pentagonal prism

Face recognition

Each of these 3-D shapes is made up of different 2-D shapes. Your challenge is to line up the seven shapes so that each one shares a 2-D shape with the 3-D shape that follows it. So, for example, a cube can be followed by a square pyramid, because they both contain a 2-D square. The faces do not have to be the same size.

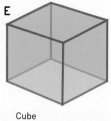
E

Cube

F

Triangular prism

G

Square pyramid

Did you know that the shape of a doughnut is an official 3-D shape, called a torus? Yum!

Trace a trail

Can you follow all the edges of these 3-D shapes without going over the same line twice? Try drawing each of the shapes without lifting your pen. You'll only be able to do this for one shape, but which is it? And can you figure out why?

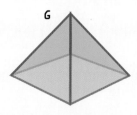
A

Octahedron

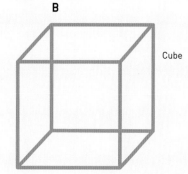
B

Cube

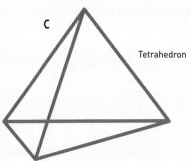
C

Tetrahedron

Building blocks

Using the single cube as a guide, can you visualize how many would fit into each of the larger 3-D shapes? If the the single cube represents 1 cubic centimeter (cm³), what is the volume of each shape?

This cube represents 1 cm³

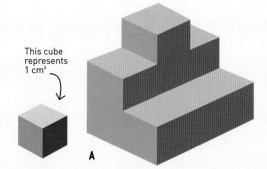
A

B

3-D FUN

Explore the remarkable strength of egg-shaped domes, and turn 2-D pieces of paper into 3-D objects with a little cutting and folding.

Tough eggs

The dome is a popular shape for buildings because it can support a surprisingly large weight, as this egg-speriment proves.

You will need:
- Four eggs
- Clear tape
- Pencil
- Scissors
- A stack of heavy books

Step 1

Carefully tap the pointy end of an egg on a hard surface to break the shell. The rest of the egg must be unbroken. Pour out the contents of the egg.

Step 2

Stick clear tape around the middle of the egg. Draw a line around the widest part and ask an adult to score it with scissors.

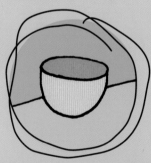

Step 3

Gently break off pieces of the shell from the pointy end to the line, then use the scissors to snip around the line. If the shell beyond the line cracks, start again. Prepare three more eggs this way.

Step 4

Set out your four eggs in a rectangular shape. Carefully place a stack of heavy books on top of the shells. How many books can you add before the eggshells crack?

Tetrahedron trick

Create a tetrahedron from an envelope in a few simple steps.

You will need:
- Envelope
- Pencil
- Scissors
- Clear tape

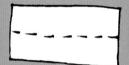

Step 1

Seal the envelope and fold it in half lengthwise to make a crease along the middle.

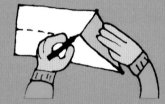

Step 2

Fold down one corner until it touches the center fold. Make a mark at this point.

Step 3

Unfold the corner, draw a vertical line through the point you marked, then cut along it.

Step 4

Using the smaller part of the envelope, fold it from the mark to each corner, creasing the fold on both sides.

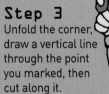
Open edge

Step 5

Put your hand in the open side and open up the tetrahedron, taping together the open edges.

Your tetrahedron should open up neatly along the creases

Fold a cube

Here's how to transform a flat piece of paper into a solid cube. To make a water bomb, fill it with water through the hole in the top!

You will need:
- Pencil
- Square of paper

Step 1
Fold the paper in half along both diagonals. Then unfold and turn over.

Step 2
Now fold the paper in half along both horizontals. Add labels, as shown.

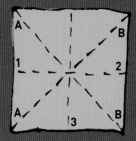

A   B
1   2
A   B
3

Step 3
Fold points 1 and 2 onto 3, A to A, and B to B, so the paper becomes a triangle.

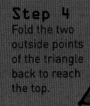

Fold neatly to create a triangle

1 2
3

Step 4
Fold the two outside points of the triangle back to reach the top.

Make sure the corners and edges are flush

Step 5
Turn the paper over and repeat step 4.

Step 6
Fold the side points into the center.

Step 7
Fold down the top edges and tuck them into the triangular pockets. Turn over and repeat steps 6 and 7.

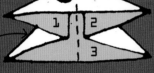

Step 8
Gently pull the edges out and blow into the hole in one end to create a cube.

As soon as you start to blow, the cube will inflate

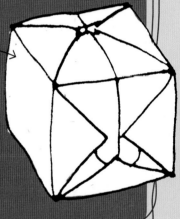

Walk through paper

Tell your friends that you can walk through paper. They won't believe you, but here is the secret...

You will need:
- Pencil
- Sheet of letter-sized paper
- Scissors

Step 1
Draw this pattern onto the sheet of paper and cut along the lines.

Step 2
Carefully open the sheet of paper and amaze your friends as you step through the large hole.

Leonhard Euler

Leonhard Euler was an extraordinary man whose knowledge included many apects of math and physics. He developed new ideas, which were used to explain, for example, the movement of many different objects—from sailing ships to planets. Euler had a particular gift of being able to "see" the answer to problems. During his life, he published more papers on math than anyone else—and could also recite a 10,000-line poem from memory.

The Academy of Science in St. Petersburg was set up to improve Russian education and science, so that the country could compete academically with the rest of Europe.

To Russia with love

Euler was born in 1707 in Switzerland, and soon devoted himself to mathematics. After graduating from the University of Basel, he moved to Russia to join Empress Catherine I's Academy of Science. The academy had been founded three years earlier with help from the German mathematician Gottfried Leibniz. Just six years after his arrival, Euler took over from another Swiss mathematician, Daniel Bernoulli, as the academy's head of mathematics.

Euler's rule

Long ago, the Ancient Greeks discovered five regular shapes called Platonic solids. Two thousand years later, Euler found that they obey a simple rule: The number of corners plus the number of faces minus the edges always equals 2.

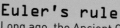

Face (f)

Edge (e)

Tetrahedron

Corner, also known as a vertex (v)

	v		f		e		
Tetrahedron	4	+	4	-	6	=	2
Cube	8	+	6	-	12	=	2
Octahedron	6	+	8	-	12	=	2
Dodecahedron	20	+	12	-	30	=	2
Icosahedron	12	+	20	-	30	=	2

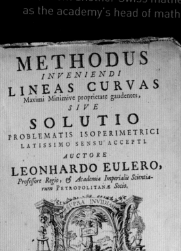

Math and physics

With books such as *A Method for Finding Curved Lines*, Euler used math to solve problems of physics. He wrote more than 800 papers in his life. After his death, it took 35 years to publish them all. Euler even has his own number—2.71818..., known as "e" or Euler's number.

It is claimed that Euler once upset a famous philosopher by "proving" that God exists, saying, "Sir, $a + b^n/n = x$, therefore God exists..."

On the move

In the 1730s, Russia was a violent and dangerous place, and Euler retreated into the world of math. In 1741, he moved to the Berlin Academy of Science to try his hand at philosophy—but he did so badly that he was replaced. When Catherine I of Russia offered him the directorship of the St. Petersburg Academy in 1766, Euler accepted and spent the rest of his life in Russia.

Euler was pictured on the Swiss 10-franc banknote and on many Swiss, German, and Russian postage stamps.

The old Prussian city of Königsberg is now called Kalingrad, in Russia, and its seven bridges are now five.

The Prussian problem

In 1735, Euler put forward an answer to the so-called Königsberg bridge problem. The city's River Pregel contained two islands that could be reached by seven bridges. Was there a route around the city that crossed each bridge only once? Instead of using trial and error, Euler found a way to answer the question that gave rise to a new area of math called graph theory. His answer was that no such route was possible.

A life of genius

Half blind for much of his life, Euler lost his sight completely soon after his return to St. Petersburg. He was so brilliant at mental arithmetic, however, that this had no effect on his work. When Euler was 60 years old, he was awarded a prize for working out how the gravities of the Earth, Sun, and Moon affect each other. On the day he died, September 18, 1783, Euler was working out the laws of motion of hot-air balloons.

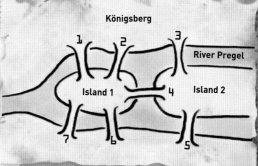

Königsberg

River Pregel

Island 1   Island 2

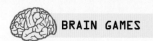

Simple mazes

There's a very easy way to solve mazes that have all the walls connected, such as this one. You simply put one of your hands on the wall and keep it there as you go—it doesn't matter which hand, but don't change hands along the way. As you'll discover, this isn't the fastest route, but you'll always end up at the exit.

The world's largest maze was opened in the town of Fontanellato, Italy, in 2012. The bamboo-hedge design is based on mazes shown in Roman mosaics.

AMAZING MAZES

People have been fascinated by mazes for thousands of years. One of the most famous is the mythical Greek labyrinth of Crete, which had a monster lurking inside. Mathematicians in particular have always loved exploring mazes, for working out solutions to seemingly hard problems, and of course for fun.

Complex mazes

Mazes such as this one, where not all the walls are connected, cannot be solved using the one-hand rule (see top of page). You'll just end up going around and around in circles. Instead, you have to try and memorize your route, or leave a trail to show which paths you've been down.

Make a Cretan maze

Created more than 3,200 years ago, the Cretan labyrinth was a very simple unicursal (one-path) maze. You couldn't get lost, but you never knew what lay around the next bend. Here's how to draw your own.

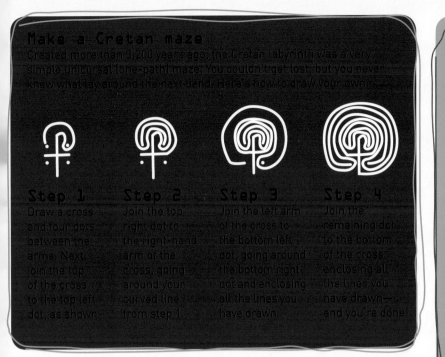

Step 1
Draw a cross and four dots between the arms. Next, join the top of the cross to the top left dot, as shown.

Step 2
Join the top right dot to the right-hand arm of the cross, going around your curved line from step 1.

Step 3
Join the left arm of the cross to the bottom left dot, going around the bottom right dot and enclosing all the lines you have drawn.

Step 4
Join the remaining dot to the bottom of the cross, enclosing all the lines you have drawn— and you're done!

Weave maze

Seen from above, this mind-bending puzzle resembles a 3-D maze. Passages weave under and over each other, like tunnels or bridges. Although a passage never ends under or over another path, you still need to watch out for dead ends in other parts of the maze.

Mazes as networks

It is possible to turn a complex maze into a simple diagram, called a network. Marking only the junction points and dead ends and linking these with short lines reveals the direct route through the maze.

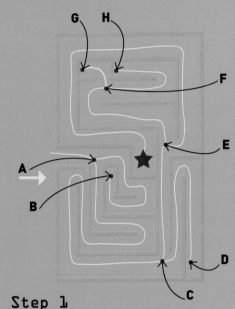

Step 1
Mark every junction and every dead end in the maze, and give each a different letter, as shown above. The order of the letters doesn't matter. Join the points with lines to show all possible routes.

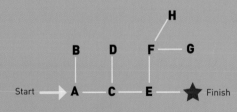

Step 2
Write down the letters and join them with short lines to get a diagram of the maze in its simplest form. Maps of underground train systems are usually laid out like this, making routes easier to plan.

Electronic networks

Network diagrams have many uses. In an electronic circuit, for instance, what really matters is that the components are connected correctly. A network diagram of the circuit is much simpler to draw and check than one that takes account of the actual positions of the components.

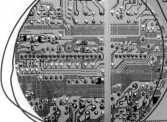

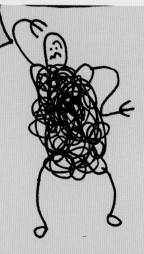

Perspective play

Looking down a path going into the distance, we assume that people or objects will appear smaller as they move farther away. In this photo, your brain interprets the person farthest away as a giantess, compared to the figures behind her. In reality, all three images are the same size.

OPTICAL ILLUSIONS

The brain uses visual evidence from the eyes to figure out what we're seeing. To do this, it uses all kinds of clues, such as colors and shapes. By making pictures with misleading clues, the brain can be tricked.

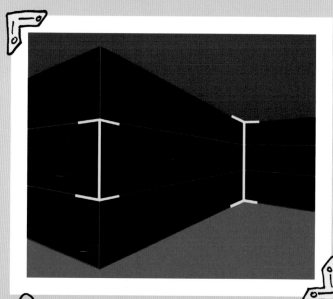

Filling in the gaps

We rarely see the whole of an object—usually, parts are obscured and the brain guesses what we're seeing and fills in the missing sections. Here, the brain fills things in to show you a white triangle that isn't really there.

Bigger or smaller?

Your brain tries to recognize shapes. In the image above, your brain thinks you are looking at three rectangular sections of a wall from an angle. Taking the wall as a clue, the yellow bar on the right must surely be farther away than the one on the left? It must also be longer, since it spans the whole wall. But try measuring both...

Young or old?

Your brain cannot help but try to work out what an image shows. Here, there is equal evidence that we are seeing an old woman and a young one. It depends on where you look. If you focus in the middle, you are likely to see the old woman's eye, but look to the left and the eye becomes the young woman's ear.

Making waves

Believe it or not, all the lines of the shapes below are straight. Your brain is tricked into seeing wavy lines because of the position of the tiny black and white squares in the corners of the larger squares.

Color confusion

Our brain makes adjustments to the way colors appear in different lighting conditions, because it "knows" the colors are fixed. Here, the brain sees square B and gives you the information that the square is light gray, but in shadow. In fact, square B is the same color as A!

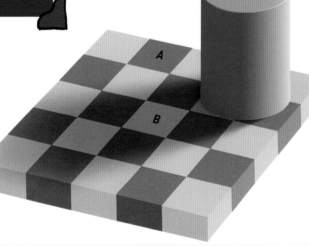

IMPOSSIBLE SHAPES

When we look at an object, each eye sees a 2-D image, which the brain puts together to make a 3-D image. But sometimes, the 2-D images can trick the brain, which then comes up with the wrong answer, and we "see" impossible objects.

Freaky fence

Cover first one post, and then the other. Both images make sense. View the whole image together, however, and the shape is impossible. Pictures such as this one are made by combining pairs of images, where each is taken from a different angle.

The international recycling symbol, symbolizing an endless cycle, is base on the Möbius strip

Penrose triangle

The Penrose triangle is named after Roger Penrose, the physicist who made it famous. If you cover any side of the triangle, it looks like a normal shape, but put the three sides together and the whole thing makes no sense.

Crazy crate

Sometimes, an impossible object can be turned into a possible one by making a simple change. This crate would make perfect sense if you redrew the upright bar, seen here to the left of the man, so that it passed behind the horizontal bar at the front.

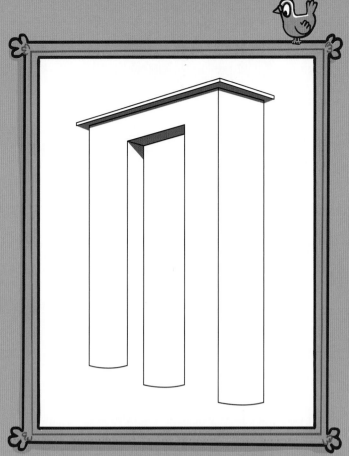

Mathematicians don't just study real shapes and spaces, they are also able to explore imaginary worlds in which space and geometry are different.

Impossible?

Although this shape looks as strange as the others on this page, it is actually the only one that really exists—and it does not need to be viewed from a particular angle, either. Can you figure out how it's made? There's a clue somewhere on this page.

Fantasy fork

The three prongs of this fork make no sense if you follow them up to see how they meet at the top. But cover the top or bottom half of it, and both ends look fine. The illusion works because there is no background. If you tried coloring in the background, you would get really confused!

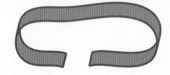

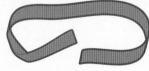

Strange strip

The Möbius strip, discovered in 1858, is a most unusual shape. For a start, it has only one surface and one edge. Don't believe it? Make a strip for yourself and then run a highlighter along an outside edge and see what happens.

Step 1

All you need to create a Möbius strip is paper and glue or tape. Cut a long strip of paper. It should be about 12 in (30 cm) long and 1.5 in (3 cm) wide.

Step 2

Give one end of your strip of paper a single twist, then use a dab of glue or a piece of tape to join the two ends of the paper strip together.

Step 3

To see if the strip really does have only one surface, draw a line along the center of the strip. Now cut along this line—you may be surprised by the result.

A world of

INTERESTING TIMES

Everyone knows what time is, but try putting it into words. Whatever it is, we use time for all kinds of things, from boiling an egg or catching a bus to knowing when to blow the whistle at a soccer game. Extra time, anyone?

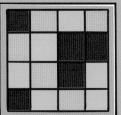

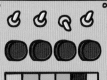

Dividing time
The Egyptians were the first to divide the day into 24 hours, but their hours were not all the same length. To make sure that there were always 12 hours from sunrise to sunset, they made the hours longer during summer days and winter nights.

The clocks show how many hours behind or ahead of Greenwich, England, each time zone is.

Crossing continents
Russia stretches from Europe to Asia and crosses 9 time zones.

Greenwich Meridian

The poles
Time zones meet at the North and South Poles. By walking around the points of the poles, you can travel through all the time zones in a few seconds.

Lengths of time
- Millennium (1,000 years)
- Century (100 years)
- Decade (10 Years)
- Leap year (366 days)
- Year (365 days)
- Month (28, 29, 30, or 31 days)
- Lunar month (about 29.5 days)
- Fortnight (14 days)
- Week (7 days)
- Day (24 hours)
- Hour (60 minutes)
- Minute (60 seconds)
- Second (basic unit of time)
- Millisecond (thousandth of a second)
- Microsecond (millionth of a second)
- Nanosecond (billionth of a second)

Natural units
Although exact times are based on the second, we also use three units based on natural events:
- A day is one rotation of the Earth on its axis.
- A lunar month is one full cycle of the Moon.
- A year is the time it takes Earth to orbit the Sun.

Time zones

The world is divided into 24 time zones, with the time in each zone measured in hours ahead of or behind the Greenwich Meridian. This is the imaginary line at 0° longitude that joins the North and South Poles and passes through Greenwich, England. On the opposite side of the Earth, at 180° longitude, is the International Date Line. This imaginary line separates two different calendar days.

International Date Line

Time travel
In 2011, Samoa shifted the International Date Line from its west coast to its east coast, skipping Friday, December 30, altogether!

Super-accurate

Most modern clocks contain a quartz crystal that sends out a regular pulse of electricity, and use this to keep time. They are accurate to a few seconds a year. The world's most accurate clocks rely on the lengths of light waves from metal atoms and would not lose a second in a billion years.

Light-years

Light-years are a measure of distance, not time. One light-year is the distance light travels in one year, about 5.88 trillion miles (9.46 trillion km).

Your body clock runs faster when your brain is hot, such as when you have a fever.

ACTIVITY

Body clock

Humans have a built-in sense of time, or "body clock." It is driven by the rhythms of the day, such as light and darkness. If you fly across several time zones, it can get very confused and you may suffer from jet lag. Why don't you test your sense of time? Before you go to sleep, set your mind to wake you up at a particular time the next morning. When you wake up, check yourself against a clock. You'll almost certainly wake up on time.

MAPPING

Maps are a way of showing information as pictures or shapes. The most familiar ones help us find our way, representing streets and landscapes using words, symbols, and colors to give as much information as possible. These maps are usually "to scale." This means that a fixed distance on the map represents a fixed distance in the real world.

Contours

A map is flat but a hill isn't, so how can we show a hill on a map? The answer is to use contour lines. These connect all the points that are the same height above sea level. One contour line, for example, goes through every point at a height of 30 ft (10 m), one through the points at 40 ft (15 m), and so on.

Maps of everything

A map is a way of showing information in pictures so that it's easier to understand. There are maps for all kinds of things—a flow diagram is a way to map the process for building a car, for example. Not all maps are to scale—a map of the subway, for example. And a mind map is a way of showing how our brains come up with ideas.

Even on a scale map, not everything is to scale. For instance, roads are nearly always drawn wider, so that their details are clear.

GPS support

Finding out where you are on a map can be tricky—but using a GPS (Global Positioning System) device can help. Using information from satellites, it finds your exact location, displays it on a map, and can even give you directions.

Locations as numbers

Landscape maps feature a grid of numbered lines. The horizontal lines run from south to north, and the vertical lines move from west to east, and the square where the lines 45 and 01 cross is at grid reference 4501. A parking lot in the square where the lines 45 and 01 cross is at grid reference 4501. This can also be written as "45 east, 1 north," or as map coordinates: 45,01.

ACTIVITY

On the map

Looking at the map, can you figure out the coordinates for the church and the campsite?

Contour lines

Understanding scale

Since landscape maps are a representation of an area, things need to be in the right places, and the right distances apart. To make the map small enough to be useful, the image has to be scaled down, so that everything is made smaller in the same proportion. A typical street map might have a scale of 1 in to 1,000 ft. In other words, an inch on the map represents 1,000 ft in the real world. The scale is written as 1:12,000, since 1,000 ft is equal to 12,000 in.

Scale 1:12,000

10 Miles

15 Kilometers

0   5   10

0   5   10

35
30
25
20
15
10
05

Grace Hopper

Math professor and naval officer Grace Hopper was a pioneer of computer science. Her trailblazing work in developing computer languages, programming, and software led to computers coming out of specialist science labs and into the wider world, becoming essential in virtually every office, classroom, and home.

The IBM Automated Sequence Controlled Calculator, also known as the Harvard Mark I, was the first computer capable of doing automatic calculations.

War work

In 1943, Grace Hopper left her job as a math professor to enlist in the US Navy and help the US fight in World War II. She worked on one of the world's first computers, the massive, room-sized Harvard Mark I. One of the first three people with the job title of "coder" (now called programmer), Hopper wrote the first-ever computer manual—a top-secret text on how to write codes to calculate rocket trajectories and make computing tables for the design of torpedoes and underwater detection systems.

UNIVAC I

After the war, Hopper helped build the Universal Automatic Computer (UNIVAC I), the first commercial all-electronic computer. The gigantic machine had 200 miles (322 km) of wiring and 5,000 tubes. More than 46 UNIVAC machines were sold. In the 1960s, NASA used later UNIVAC hardware to communicate with the astronauts on the *Apollo* moon missions.

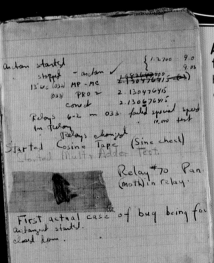

A bug in the system

Hopper often gets the credit for coming up with the term "bug" to describe a computer glitch, and although earlier engineers had already coined the term, she was the one who made it famous. In 1947, when her machine began to malfunction, the team found a moth lodged in the computer's circuits. Hopper put the moth in her diary and wrote "first actual case of bug being found!"

A new language

During the 1950s, Hopper realized the need for a common programming language that could be used on different computers. She invented a way of using human language to talk to computers to make it easier for businesses and non-mathematicians to operate them. This meant that, instead of entering mathematical formulae or symbols, a person could type a command in English. She called this language COBOL (Common Business Oriented Language), and it went on to transform how computers were used.

A long career

Throughout her career in the computer industry, Hopper remained a Navy reservist, and finally retired at the age of 79 as a rear admiral. In 1997, the Navy launched a new, high-tech destroyer, the USS *Hopper*, named in her honor. In 1992, she was awarded the US's highest honor in her field, the National Medal of Technology and in 2016, more than a decade after her death, she was awarded the Presidential Medal of Freedom.

High-level Language
print//: _"hello"_

Compiler

Machine Code:
```
110100101101011010010100010101
001101111101101000111010101011010
010101010101010100101010101011010
100101101011010110101010100010
011010101101010100010101010011
011100110101001011110110011101
```

Computer compiler

In 1952, Hopper's team developed A-0—an early version of something called a "compiler." The compiler worked by helping to translate a programming language, which contained words and mathematical symbols, into a machine-readable code known as binary code, made up of only the digits 1 and 0.

PROBABILITY

Probability is the branch of math that deals with the chance that something will happen. Mathematicians express probability using a number from zero to one. A probability of zero means that something definitely won't happen, while a probability of one means that it definitely will. Anything in-between is something that may happen and can be calculated as a fraction or percentage of one.

What are the chances?

Working out chances is quite simple. First, you need to count the number of possible outcomes. The chance of throwing a die and getting a four is one in six ($\frac{1}{6}$), because there are six ways for the die to fall, just one of which is the four. The chances of throwing an odd number (1, 3, or 5) is one in two ($\frac{3}{6} = \frac{1}{2}$) or 50 percent.

How chance adds up

The chance of a tossed coin being a head is $\frac{1}{2}$ (one in two). The chances of a head then a tail is $\frac{1}{2} \times \frac{1}{2} = \frac{1}{4}$. The chances of a head then another head (which can be written HH to save space) is also $\frac{1}{4}$. The chances of three tails in a row (TTT) is $\frac{1}{2} \times \frac{1}{2} \times \frac{1}{2} = \frac{1}{8}$.

1st toss	2nd toss	3rd toss
		$\frac{1}{2}$ H
	$\frac{1}{2}$ H	$\frac{1}{2}$ T
		$\frac{1}{2}$ H
$\frac{1}{2}$ H	$\frac{1}{2}$ T	$\frac{1}{2}$ T
		$\frac{1}{2}$ H
	$\frac{1}{2}$ H	$\frac{1}{2}$ T
$\frac{1}{2}$ T		$\frac{1}{2}$ H
	$\frac{1}{2}$ T	$\frac{1}{2}$ T

chance: $\frac{1}{2}$ chance: $\frac{1}{4}$ chance: $\frac{1}{8}$

But don't risk it!

It's tempting to think that if you have tossed four heads in a row, the next toss is more likely to be a head. But it's equally likely to be a tail: The chance of HHHHT is $\frac{1}{2} \times \frac{1}{2} \times \frac{1}{2} \times \frac{1}{2} \times \frac{1}{2} = \frac{1}{32}$, and the chance of HHHHH is exactly the same.

Chaos

Some things, such as where a pinball will bounce, are almost impossible to predict. Each ball you fire takes a slightly different route. Even the tiniest differences in the ball's starting position and how much you press the flipper or pull the spring become magnified into major changes in direction as the ball bounces around the table. This unpredictable behavior is called "chaotic."

The house always wins

Ever wondered how casinos make money? They make sure the chances of winning are stacked in their favor. Casino games give the "house" (the casino itself) a statistical edge that means it wins more often than it loses. For example, if you bet on a number in a game of roulette, you have a 1 in 36 chance of winning. But a roulette wheel also has a 37th space for zero. This ultimately gives the casino an advantage. It will win more games than it loses, since it doesn't pay anyone if the ball lands on the zero. It's this zero that gives the house its "edge."

The chance of a shuffled pack of cards being in the right order is less than one in a trillion trillion trillion trillion trillion.

Predictions

Using probability, you can try to predict or forecast things that are going to happen. For example, imagine you have a bag containing five red balls, six blue balls, and seven yellow balls. What color ball are you most likely to pull out—red, blue, or yellow? The answer is yellow because there are more yellow balls in the bag, so the probability is higher for this color. Predictions aren't always correct. You could pull out a red or blue ball—it's just less likely to happen.

ACTIVITY

What are the odds?

Sometimes our brain misleads us. We can be influenced by things that aren't really true. For example, books and blockbuster films lead us to believe that sharks are very dangerous to humans. In reality, however, more people are killed by hippos than sharks. Try putting these causes of death in order of probability:

- 👁 Computer game exhaustion
- 👁 Snake bite
- 👁 Hippo attack
- 👁 Walking into a lamppost
- 👁 Falling down a manhole
- 👁 Playing soccer
- 👁 Hit by a falling coconut
- 👁 Struck by lightning
- 👁 Hit by a meteorite
- 👁 Shark attack

DISPLAYING DATA

When you want to know what's going on in the world, you need the facts—or data. This will often be in the form of a lot of numbers that don't tell you much at first, but present them in the right way and you'll get the picture. Here's the latest data on superhero activity...

A crime tally

It can be tough for a superhero to decide which villain to tackle first. A simple tally of their evil deeds is a great way to see at a glance who's the worst threat to the city.

Numero

~~||||~~ ~~||||~~ ~~||||~~ ~~||||~~ |||

Pi Man

~~||||~~ ~~||||~~ ||||

Graphic picture

Using a line graph to plot data over time—like the number of crimes in your city—it's easy to spot those times when villains are in town. And if a superhero can find a pattern, it makes the job a lot easier!

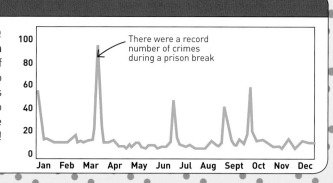

There were a record number of crimes during a prison break

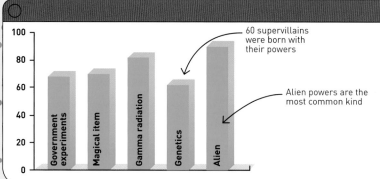

60 supervillains were born with their powers

Alien powers are the most common kind

Bar none

One way to fight tomorrow's evildoers is to find out where supervillains get their powers from and use this knowledge to beat them. A bar chart like this, where the heights of the bars show the number of supervillains with powers of a certain source, compares them at a glance.

Name	Secret identity	Sidekicks	Hero or villain	Arch-nemesis
Math Man	Yes	Yes	Hero	Numero
Calcutron	No	No	Hero	None
The Human Shape	No	Yes	Hero	None
Numero	Yes	No	Villain	Math Man
Pi Man	Yes	Yes	Villain	None

On the table

Knowing all the facts about your fellow heroes and villains can come in very handy. A simple table of information is helpful because it presents multiple facts in a clear and effective manner.

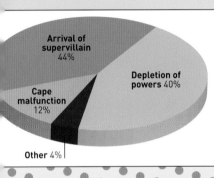

Arrival of supervillain 44%

Depletion of powers 40%

Cape malfunction 12%

Other 4%

Pie in the sky

Even superheroes can fail sometimes. What went wrong? Handy pie charts like this one, in which the area of each slice is a fraction of the whole, show the major areas for concern.

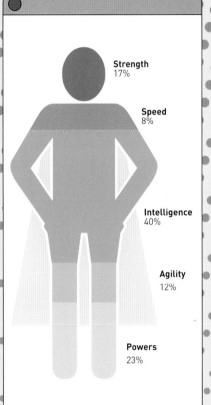

Strength 17%

Speed 8%

Intelligence 40%

Agility 12%

Powers 23%

Check it out

If you're looking to recruit new superheroes into your legion, and you need to know if they've got what it takes, a simple checklist of their powers can help you make an informed decision.

- ⊘ Flight
- ⊘ Super strength
- ⊘ Invisibility
- ⊘ Telekinesis
- ⊘ Super intelligence
- ⊘ Psychic powers

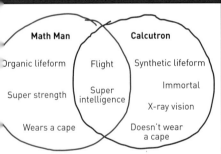
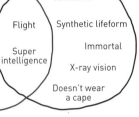

Math Man

Calcutron

Organic lifeform

Flight

Synthetic lifeform

Super strength

Super intelligence

Immortal

X-ray vision

Wears a cape

Doesn't wear a cape

Who does what?

When you put a team of superheroes together, you need a good range of skills. Venn diagrams are an ideal method of comparing characteristics and showing which are shared—and which are not.

Profile pictogram

When drawing up the profile of the perfect superhero, a pictogram is a great way to show the balance of qualities you're looking for. It combines a range of information within one fact-packed picture. Here, the depths of the coloured areas reflect the mix of qualitites.

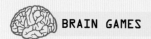
LOGIC PUZZLES
AND PARADOXES

To solve these puzzles, you need to think carefully. This area of math is called logic—you get the answer by working through the problem, step by step. But watch out, one puzzle here is a paradox, a statement that seems to be absurd or to contradict itself.

Black or white?
Amy, Beth, and Claire are wearing hats, which they know are either black or white. They also know that not all three are white. Amy can see Beth and Claire's hats, Beth can see Amy and Claire's, and Claire is blindfolded. Each is asked in turn if they know the color of their own hat. The answers are: Amy—no, Beth—no, and Claire—yes. What color is Claire's hat, and how does she know?

Logical square
Each of the colored squares below contains a different hidden number from 1–8. Using the clues, can you work out which number goes where?

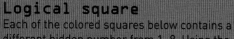

- The numbers in the dark blue and dark green squares add up to 3.
- The number in the red square is even.
- The number in the red square and the number below it add up to 10.
- The number in the light green square is twice the number in the dark green square.
- The sum of the numbers in the last column is 11 and their difference is 1.
- The number in the orange square is odd.
- The numbers in the yellow and light green squares add up to one of the numbers in the bottom row.

A barber's dilemma
A village barber cuts the hair of everybody who doesn't cut their own. But who cuts his hair?

- If he does, then he is one of those people who cuts their own hair.
- But he doesn't cut the hair of people who cut their own hair. So he doesn't cut his own hair.
- But he is the man who cuts the hair of everyone who doesn't cut their own hair.
- So he does cut his hair... which takes us back to the start again.

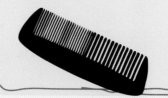

Four digits
What is the four-digit number in which the first digit is one-third of the second, the third is the sum of the first and second, and the last is three times the second?

People with pets

Four friends each have a pet. There's a cat, a fish, a dog, and a parrot. The pets' names are Nibbles, Buttons, Snappy, and Goldy. From what the friends are saying below, can you figure out who has which pet, and the names of each animal?

Cat   Fish   Dog   Parrot

Anna: My pet isn't a goldfish or a dog, but it is named Nibbles.

Bob: My pet is named Buttons and likes swimming.

Dave: I don't have a dog...

Dave: ...and I know Goldy is a cat.

Cecilia: I'm allergic to fur, so my pet doesn't have any, and my pet has the second shortest name of the four.

If you're having trouble, try drawing a grid with the people's names in the first column, and then filling in any clues you've worked out.

Lost at sea

It's a foggy gray day at sea and, viewed from the air, you can only make out some empty blue water and parts of ships. Can you find out where the rest of the fleet is located? Every ship is surrounded on all sides by squares of empty water.

Fleet:

6 Dinghies:

4 Yachts:

2 Cruisers:

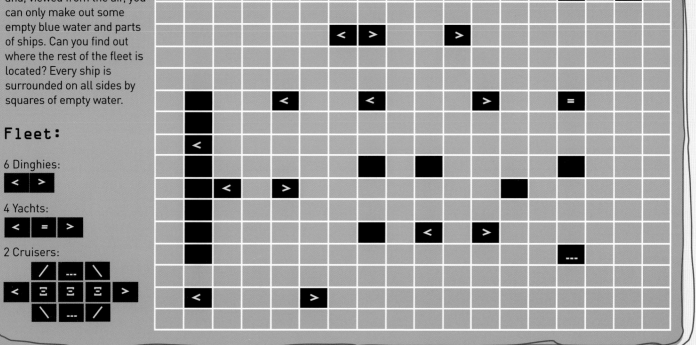

Charles Babbage

The English mathematician Babbage (1791–1871) was a champion code breaker. In 1854, he broke a famous military cipher that used 26 alphabets to encipher each message. This discovery was used to decipher Russian messages during the Crimean War. Babbage invented the first true computer, and although it was not built in his lifetime, English mathematician Ada Lovelace had written what we would now call its program—the first in the world.

Thomas Jefferson

A decade before he became president, Jefferson (1743–1826) invented a revolutionary coding machine called a "wheel cypher." He went on to oversee and develop several other ciphers, too. They were used to send messages to Europe and to keep in touch with secret missions. The U.S. military adopted Jefferson's wheel ciphers, using them from 1922 until 1942.

Agnes Meyer Driscoll

Driscoll (1889–1971) was one of the best code breakers of the 20th century. Working for the U.S. Navy, she broke some of the most difficult codes of the time, including many of those used in the world wars. Sometimes known as "Madame X," Driscoll also helped develop code-breaking machines and teach other code breakers.

Sir Francis Walsingham

During the reign of Elizabeth I of England, spying was widespread. Walsingham (c. 1532–90) was a master spy. He discovered an assassination plot by Elizabeth's cousin, Mary, Queen of Scots, by intercepting Mary's messages. His code-breaking expertise led to Mary's execution.

ACTIVITY

Codes everywhere

There are codes all around us, and many of them are designed to be read by machines. If you have a smartphone, there will be at least one "bar code scanner" app for it. You can use this to read the bar codes of all kinds of products in stores or even just items on your kitchen shelves. See what information comes up about them. Try using it to scan library books, too.

BREAKING CODES

If you have a secret message to read, call in the experts! Both codes and ciphers make readable messages unreadable, and both can be cracked using math. Codes change each word to a code word, symbol, or number. Ciphers jumble the letters or replace them with different symbols.

Hacker

A hacker is someone who breaks into computer systems, either just for fun or to steal valuable information. Hacking into a computer system often involves decrypting (decoding) computer code or messages. Sometimes, hackers are employed by computer companies to test their systems and make them more secure. These hackers are sometimes nicknamed "white-hat hackers."

To test security, an IBM employee named Scott Lunsford tried to hack into the computer system of a nuclear power plant. It took him just a day.

Public key encryption

One big math breakthrough of the early 1970s was public key encryption. A key is the name for the information needed to make or decode a cipher. Used for all e-mails and texts, this system means that only the intended recipient can read the message. The way it works is that the recipient's computer system invents a pair of keys: one to encrypt and one to decrypt. The sender uses the encrypt key to encrypt a message to the recipient. This message can be read only by the recipient because only he or she has the decrypt key to unlock its contents.

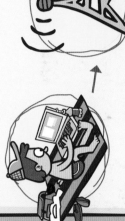

Encryption

Financial transactions are almost always sent by computer, and they need to be kept secret so that no one can steal information about the sender's or receiver's bank accounts. The transactions travel through the Internet, along wires, and through space as radio signals. Since these messages are easy to tap, they are turned into ciphers, or encrypted, for their journeys.

Frequency analysis

Simple ciphers can be broken by frequency analysis (counting how often each symbol occurs). Each symbol stands for a letter in the original text (the plaintext), so the most common symbols should represent the most common letters. In English, the most common letters are E and T, in German they're T and A, and in Spanish they're E and A. By substituting these letters for their encrypted versions, the plaintext can be worked out.

```
adf
sla sdlfk
jfdsl eowi
nfas afdslncn
hdsf hdsfkh
hfdhtjn hf eui
bcnkb hckuue cbkj
sn seh ifeuw euin
kjcntk hf dis
tnv eh
```

CODES AND CIPHERS

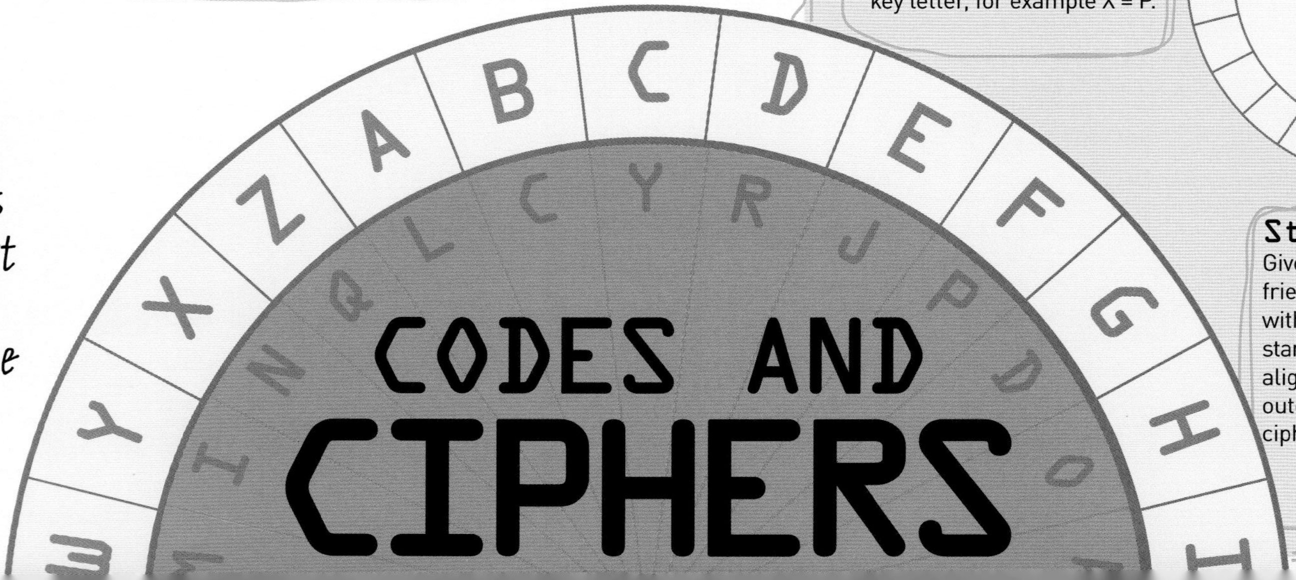

Make a cipher wheel

To write and decode a substitution cipher easily, you need a cipher wheel. Both you and the person you are sending the message to need one, and you both need to know the key to the letter substitution.

You will need:
- Paper
- Scissors
- Paper fastener
- Pencil
- Ruler

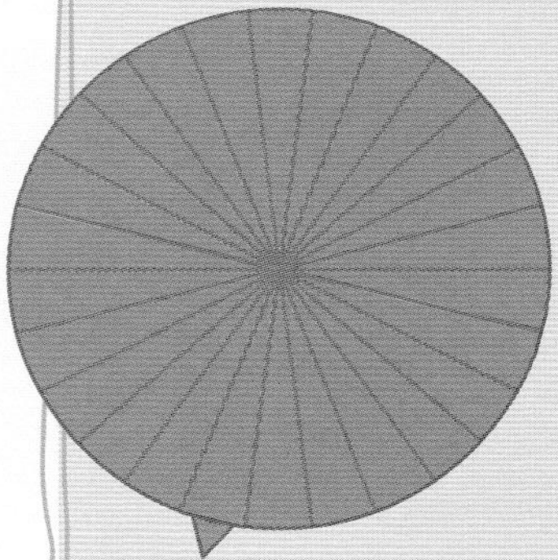

Step 1
Copy the two wheels shown here and cut them out. Put the smaller one on top, divide them both into 26 equal parts as marked, and fasten them together in the middle.

Step 2
In the outer circle write the alphabet in the correct order, and in the inner circle write the cipher alphabet (you can use the one at left, or make your own). Decide on a key letter, for example X = P.

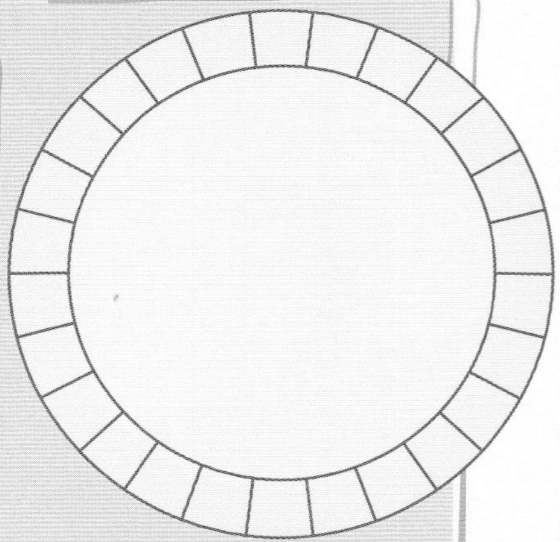

Step 3
Give the wheel to a friend and provide them with the key letter as a starting point. When they align the inner X to the outer P, the rest of the cipher will be revealed.

Caesar cipher

The Caesar cipher is named after the Roman General Julius Caesar and is a code based on substitution—replacing one letter of the alphabet with another. For example, you could replace each letter with the one that follows it, so "b" becomes "c", "c" becomes "d", and so on. In trickier versions, the letters might be two or three steps ahead, so "a" would be "d", and "b" would be "e". Can you can decipher the following message:

ZHOO GRQH WKLV LV D KDUG FRGH

💡 To figure out what the letter-gap is, think about what the one-letter word might be.

Substitution cipher

In a Caesar cipher, the coded alphabet runs in order. In a substitution cipher, it's just the position that changes. In a substitution cipher, however, the coded alphabet is not in order. Using the cipher below, what does this message say?

A	B	C	D	E	F	G	H	I	J	K	L	M	N	O	P	Q	R	S	T	U	V	W	X	Y	Z
L	C	Y	R	J	P	D	O	A	V	Z	H	B	K	T	X	G	S	W	U	F	E	M	I	N	Q

Look for Y in the bottom row, and then look above it to see which letter it really is—C

YTRJWJYLKCJPFK

Caesar's cipher might have been simple, but it was effective because at the time people weren't used to the idea of codes.

Here are some codes and ciphers for you two make and break. There are also instructions for making a cipher wheel that will make it easy for you and your friends to turn messages into top secret text.

Shape code

Each of the 11 colored shapes stands for a number between 0 and 12. Can you work out the value of each shape using math and logic?

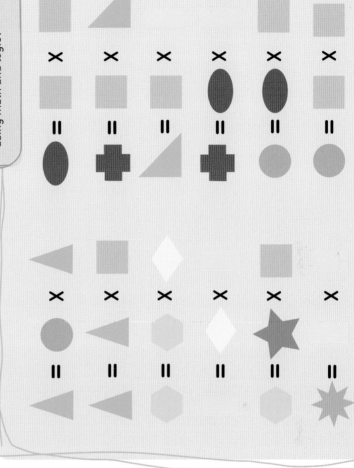

Start by thinking about which numbers could make this equation work

Polybius cipher

Polybius (c. 200–118 BCE) was a Greek historian who worked for the Romans and devised a new kind of cipher. An English version would look like the one below. To use it, you take the pair of numbers that represents each letter in the message. H is in row 2, column 3, so its ciphered number is 23.

	1	2	3	4	5
1	A	B	C	D	E
2	F	G	H	I	J
3	K	L	M	N	O
4	P	Q	R	S	T
5	U	V	W	X	YZ

Step 1
Using the cipher above, decode the following message. The letters all run together, making it trickier.

45 23 24 44 24 44 11 52 15

43 55 35 35 32 14 13 35 14 15

Step 2
Give a copy of the cipher to a friend and send each other hidden messages. You can also create your own cipher by mixing up the order of the letters—just be sure that everybody has the same cipher!

British prime minister Winston Churchill once said that Turing's work shortened World War II by two years.

A young Turing as a student at Sherborne School in Dorset, UK

Alan Turing

It was Alan Turing's brilliant mathematical mind that helped the Allies win World War II by developing new types of code-breaking machines. He then went on to build some of the world's first computers, and was a pioneer in the development of intelligent machines, the science we now call artificial intelligence.

Early life
Turing was born in London on June 23, 1912. His father worked as a civil servant in India, and not long afterward his parents returned there, leaving Turing and his older brother in the care of family friends in England. As a boy, Turing excelled at math and science. At the age of 16, he came across the work of the great scientist Albert Einstein and became fascinated by his big ideas.

The Turing machine
In 1931, Turing went to King's College, Cambridge, to study mathematics. It was here that he published a paper in 1936 about an imaginary device that carried out mathematical operations by reading and writing on a long strip of paper. Later known as a "Turing machine," his idea described how a computer could work long before the technology existed to build one. Later the same year, Turing went to the United States to study at Princeton University.

King's College, part of Cambridge University, where Turing studied from 1931. The computer room at the college is named after him.

Code-cracking
Turing returned to England in 1938, where the British government asked him to work on deciphering German codes. When World War II broke out, Turing moved to Bletchley Park, the secret headquarters of the Code and Cipher School. With his colleague Gordon Welchman, Turing developed the "Bombe," a machine that could decipher German messages encrypted (coded) on a typewriter-like device called the Enigma machine (right).

Turing was a world-class marathon runner. He came in fifth in the qualifying heats for the 1948 Olympic Games.

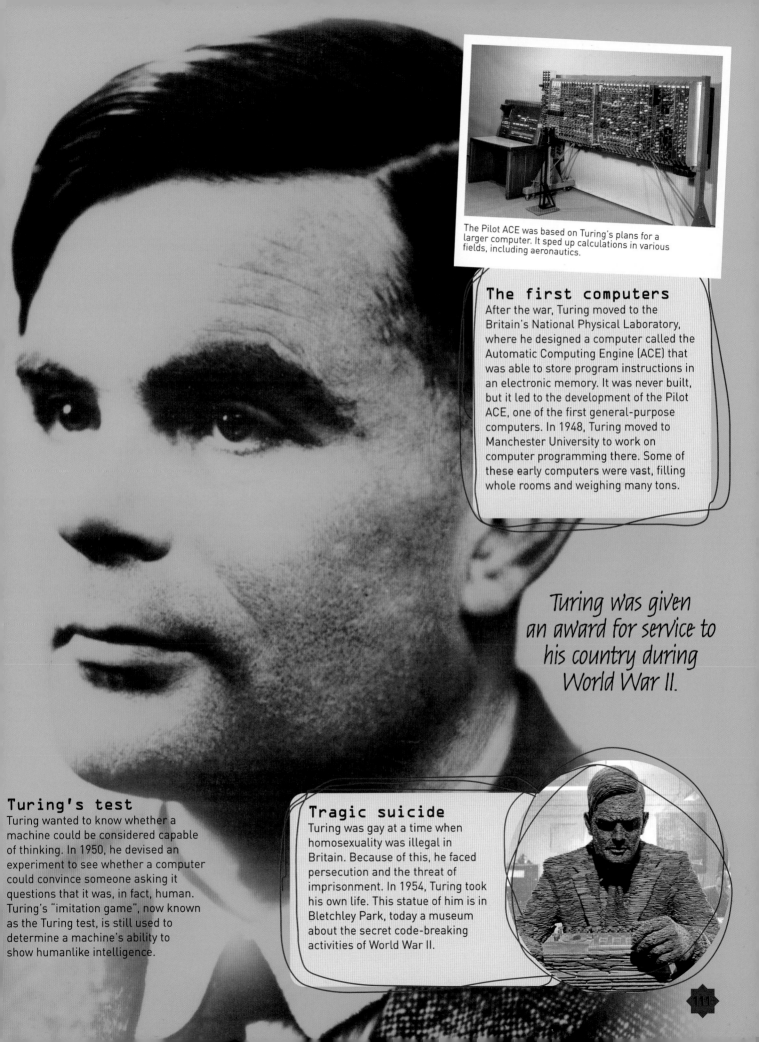

The Pilot ACE was based on Turing's plans for a larger computer. It sped up calculations in various fields, including aeronautics.

The first computers

After the war, Turing moved to the Britain's National Physical Laboratory, where he designed a computer called the Automatic Computing Engine (ACE) that was able to store program instructions in an electronic memory. It was never built, but it led to the development of the Pilot ACE, one of the first general-purpose computers. In 1948, Turing moved to Manchester University to work on computer programming there. Some of these early computers were vast, filling whole rooms and weighing many tons.

Turing was given an award for service to his country during World War II.

Turing's test

Turing wanted to know whether a machine could be considered capable of thinking. In 1950, he devised an experiment to see whether a computer could convince someone asking it questions that it was, in fact, human. Turing's "imitation game", now known as the Turing test, is still used to determine a machine's ability to show humanlike intelligence.

Tragic suicide

Turing was gay at a time when homosexuality was illegal in Britain. Because of this, he faced persecution and the threat of imprisonment. In 1954, Turing took his own life. This statue of him is in Bletchley Park, today a museum about the secret code-breaking activities of World War II.

ALG3BRA

There's an important area of math called algebra that replaces numbers with symbols (often letters of the alphabet) in order to solve a problem. In addition to mathematicians, scientists use algebra to find out things about the world.

Simple algebra
The difference between arithmetic and algebra can be seen by writing the same calculation two ways:

In arithmetic: $4 + 5 = 5 + 4$
In algebra: $x + y = y + x$

You can tell that, in this case, $x = 4$ and $y = 5$.

The first is a simple equation. The algebra, however, gives you the rule for any numbers you want to use as x and y. You can see this in the following example:

$$x + y = z$$

If you are given the values of x and y, then you can work out what z is. So if $x = 3$ and $y = 5$:

$$3 + 5 = z$$
$$z = 8$$

Find the formula
Algebra uses formulas to solve problems. A formula is kind of like a recipe—it gives you the ingredients and tells you what to do with them. Scientists use formulas for all kinds of things. For example, having received a radio signal from a spacecraft, scientists can work out how far away the spacecraft is using the formula below. It uses the metric system, which is used internationally in science.

Distance = Time x Velocity (speed) of radio waves

Put in the information you know to get the answer.

Time—in this case the radio waves reached Earth in 10 seconds

Velocity—radio waves travel at 300,000 km/second

So the distance = 10 seconds x 300,000 km/second

Distance = 3 million km

Balancing equations
The most common type of formula is an equation. This is a mathematical statement that two things are equal. Think of equations as balancing acts—what is on one side of the "equals" sign must be the same as what's on the other. For example, the total mass of a spacecraft can be described using the equation:

total mass = rocket + capsule + fuel + equipment + crew

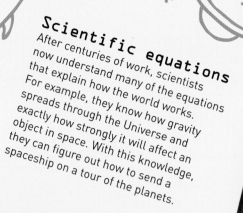

Scientific equations

After centuries of work, scientists now understand many of the equations that explain how the world works. For example, they know how gravity spreads through the Universe and exactly how strongly it will affect an object in space. With this knowledge, they can figure out how to send a spaceship on a tour of the planets.

The word "algebra" comes from the name of a book by the ancient Arab mathematician Al Khwarizimi.

Finding patterns

When there is a pattern to numbers, you can use it to figure out other information. For example, scientists on the planet Zog want to build a rocket 110 urgs (u) long and need to know how many vons of krool to use. They have this data about other rockets they have constructed:

Length	Vons of krool
30 u	140
60 u	200
80 u	240
100 u	280

The pattern that fits all the numbers above leads to the following equation:

Vons of krool = length x 2 + 80

So their new rocket would need 110 x 2 + 80 = 300 vons of krool.

Lunar lightness

Try this problem for yourself. The table below shows the weights of various objects on the Earth and on the Moon.

Object	Weight on Earth	Weight on Moon
Apple	6 oz	1 oz
Robot	300 lb	50 lb
Moon lander	18 tons	3 tons

Can you find the equation that relates weight on the Earth to weight on the Moon? How much would you weigh on the Moon?

113

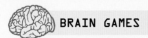
BRAINTEASERS

You use algebra to solve problems all the time—you just don't notice it. As you think through the puzzles on these pages, you'll be using algebra, but when it's disguised in everyday situations or a fun brainteaser, it's not that scary!

In algebra, "x" means an unknown number. That's why an unknown quality in a person is called "the x-factor."

Cake bake

Jim has been asked to bake a cake for a friend's birthday, and is given the following recipe:

- 16 tbsp butter
- 2 cups sugar
- 4 eggs
- 4 cups flour

At the last minute, Jim realizes that he does not have enough eggs. The stores are closed, so he decides to adapt the recipe to work with three eggs. What are the new quantities of butter, sugar, and flour he should use?

A number of petals

In each flower below, the numbers on the outside petals have been added and multiplied in the same way to make the number in the middle. Can you figure out what the pattern is, and find the answer to the third flower?

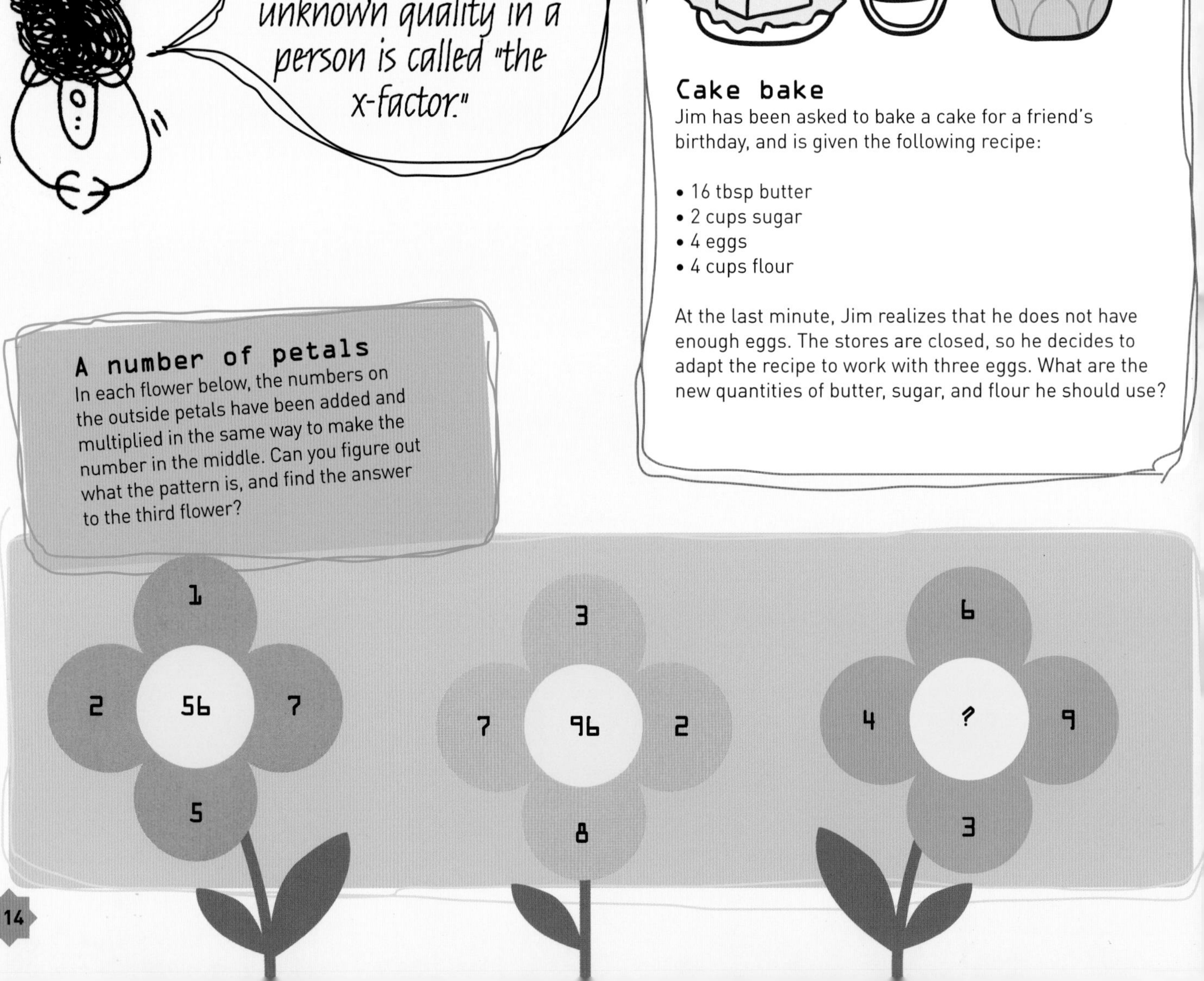

Flower 1: petals 1, 2, 7, 5 — middle 56

Flower 2: petals 3, 7, 2, 8 — middle 96

Flower 3: petals 6, 4, 9, 3 — middle ?

In a flap

There is an apple tree and a beech tree in a park, each with some birds on it. If one bird from the apple tree were to fly to the beech tree, then both trees would have the same number of birds. What is the difference between the numbers of birds?

In the balance

In math equations, you want the things on the left of an equals sign to be the same as those on the right—just as the weights on either side of a balanced scale are equal. So, in the puzzle below, how many golf balls would you need to balance the third scale?

15 golf balls

18 golf balls

A fruity challenge

Each type of fruit in these grids is worth a different number. Can you work out what the numbers are? When you have this information, figure out what the missing sum values at the end of every row and column are.

You're on your own

				71
70		**80**		

With a little help

				54
				48
			60	

Once you know what a pineapple is worth, you can then find out the value for oranges.

Start here to work out how much a pineapple is worth

SECRETS OF THE UNIVERSE

In the hands of scientists, math has the power to explain the Universe. Science is all about proving theories—and to do that, scientists need to use math to make predictions from the theory. If the predictions turn out to be correct, then the theory probably is, too.

Plant breeding project

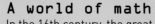

All the flowers are pink, so pink must be the dominant color

One-quarter of the flowers are white, so the pink flowers must have been carrying white flower genes

Three-quarters of the flowers are pink

A world of math

In the 16th century, the great scientist and inventor Galileo Galilei (1564–1642) discovered that many things that happen in the world can be described by simple mathematics, from falling objects and the strength of bridges to musical notes. After Galileo, nearly all scientists tried to find the mathematical laws to describe exactly how things work.

The math of life

Gregor Mendel (1822–1884), an Austrian scientist and monk, found that simple math applies to some of the characteristics of living things. Features such as flower color or eye color, for example, are always passed on from parents to offspring according to probabilities (see pages 100–101). His work was the beginning of the science of genetics.

Galileo built powerful telescopes to study astronomy, and sold others to the military for spotting enemy ships.

The simple truth

Until the early 20th century, math was used to add detail to scientific theories, to prove them, and to use them. Since then, however, math has often been used to suggest theories. When there are several theories to choose from, the one that is mathematically simplest is usually right. Genius physicist Albert Einstein (1879–1955) found the correct equations to explain gravity by choosing the simplest.

Mighty machines

Mathematicians are more likely to spend their time looking for patterns, coming up with ideas, or trying to prove new theorems than doing calculations. Why bother, when there are computers to do the work for us? The most powerful supercomputers can work billions of times faster than any human being. Their extraordinary number-crunching abilities mean scientists can test their theories more thoroughly than ever before.

Nothing's perfect

In 1931, Austrian-born mathematician Kurt Gödel (1906–1978) published a revolutionary theorem. He showed that it is impossible for any complicated mathematical theory to be complete— there will always be gaps, and there will always be statements in the theory that can't be proven. Math was never the same again!

Fields Medal-winning mathematician Maryam Mirzakhani said, "The beauty of mathematics only shows itself to more patient followers."

A world of string

One of the best theories to explain the Universe is called string theory. It says that the particles that make up atoms in the Universe are themselves made of even tinier objects that vibrate like the strings of musical instruments. This theory can only be proved mathematically because it involves things too tiny to see.

KATHERINE JOHNSON

Katherine Johnson was a mathematician who played a vital role in the US Space Program. Her achievements are even more impressive because she grew up at a time when women, especially African American women like Katherine, did not have the same opportunities as men to study and work in the field of math.

Fast learner

From childhood, Katherine was way ahead of the rest. She raced through school, starting college at just 15. She soon completed all the math courses offered, so her professors had to create more advanced programs especially for her. By the age of 18, she had already graduated in math with the highest honors. She also studied music, French, and astronomy—which would prove very useful in her chosen career.

Human computer

In 1958, Johnson got a job as a "human computer" for the US government, using math to research aircraft designs. She did so well that she was transferred to Project Mercury at the National Aeronautics and Space Administration (NASA), an ambitious mission to send a human-operated craft into orbit around the Earth and return the astronaut home safely. Katherine realized that she could use the principles of geometry to work out the paths for the spacecraft to orbit Earth.

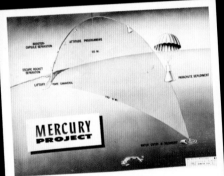

Astronaut Alan Shepard flew on the *Freedom 7* spacecraft, in the first crewed flight achieved by Project Mercury. Its trajectory is shown in this NASA artwork.

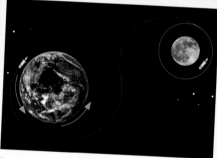

Rockets launching from Earth can use the direction Earth is spinning to help boost their speed, one of many factors that must be calculated when planning their flight path.

The math of space flight

Katherine's job on *Apollo 11* was to calculate the precise speed, acceleration, and direction required to launch the spacecraft so that it would arrive at the moon, a moving target. This was an incredibly complex task because, as well as spinning like tops, both the moon and Earth are also hurtling through space on their orbit paths—the moon around Earth, and Earth around the sun. Katherine had to plot the craft's entire flight path and accurately pinpoint where it would land on its return to Earth, so that its astronauts could be quickly recovered after splashing down in the sea.

Moon mission

In the 1960s, NASA began to use computers instead of people to work out trajectories. However, astronauts still relied on Johnson to double-check the figures and ensure their safety. Johnson worked on the *Apollo 11* mission in 1969, when Neil Armstrong became the first human to walk on the moon. She also helped prepare detailed backup navigational charts, in case of equipment failure.

The *Apollo 11* spacecraft was launched on a Saturn V rocket on July 16, 1969, from the Kennedy Space Center in Florida.

Career of a pioneer

Johnson smashed through the barriers that blocked the careers of many talented women and African American citizens. In 1939, she was one of the first three African American students in Virginia allowed on a graduate study program. When she joined NASA, she was the only woman on the team that wrote the crucial study that paved the way for the US Space Program. She produced more than 40 research papers and was NASA's foremost expert on the math of orbital flights.

Highest honors

The trajectory-planning math developed by Johnson formed the framework for NASA's modern trajectory software and modeling. Her immense contribution to math and space science was recognized in 2015 when President Barack Obama awarded her the Presidential Medal of Freedom, the United States' highest civilian honor.

GLOSSARY

algebra
The use of letters or symbols in place of numbers to study patterns in math.

angle
A measure of how far a line needs to rotate to meet another. An angle is usually measured in degrees, for example 45°.

area
The amount of space inside a 2-D shape. Area is measured in units squared, for example in^2 (cm^2).

arithmetic
Calculations that involve addition, subtraction, multiplication, or division.

axis (plural axes)
The line on a graph. The distances of points are measured from it. The horizontal axis is called the x-axis, and the vertical axis is called the y-axis.

bar graph
A type of graph that uses the heights of bars to show quantities. The higher the bar, the greater the quantity.

billion
A thousand million, or 1,000,000,000.

chart
A picture that makes mathematical information easy to understand, such as a graph, table, or map.

cipher
A code that replaces each letter with another letter, or the key to that code.

circumference
The distance around the edge of a circle.

code
A system of letters, numbers, or symbols used to replace the letters of a text to hide its meaning.

consecutive
Numbers that follow one after the other.

cube
Either a solid shape with six faces, or an instruction to multiply a number by itself three times, for example 3 x 3 x 3 = 27. This can be written 3^3.

data
Factual information, such as numbers or measurements.

decimal
A number system based on 10, using the digits 0–9. Also a number that contains a decimal place.

decimal place
The position of a digit after the decimal point.

decimal point
The dot separating the whole part of a number and the fractions of it, for example 2.5.

degrees
The unit of measurement of an angle, represented by the symbol °.

diameter
The greatest distance across a shape.

digit
A single-character number, such as 1 or 9.

encrypt
To turn a message into code to keep the information secret.

equation
A mathematical statement that two things are equal.

equilateral triangle
A triangle that has three angles of 60°, and sides of equal length.

estimate
To work out a rough answer.

even number
A number that can be divided exactly by two.

faces
The surfaces of a 3-D shape.

factors
The numbers that can be multiplied together to give a third number. For example, 2 and 4 are factors of 8.

formula
A mathematical rule, usually written in symbols.

fraction
The result of dividing one number by another.

frequency
How often something happens within a fixed period of time.

geometry
The area of math that explores shapes.

graph
A chart that shows how two sets of information are related, for example the speed and position of a moving object.

hexagon
A flat shape with six straight sides.

horizontal
Parallel to the horizon. A horizontal line runs between left and right, at right angles to the vertical. Also describes a surface that is flat, straight, and level.

isosceles triangle
A triangle with at least two sides of equal length and two equal angles.

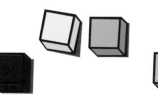

line of symmetry
If a shape has a line of symmetry, you can place a mirror along the line and the reflection will give an exact copy of half the original shape.

measurement
A number that gives the amount or size of something, written in units such as seconds or feet.

octagon
A flat shape with eight straight sides.

odd number
A number that gives a fraction with 0.5 at the end when divided by two.

parallel
Two straight lines are parallel if they are always the same distance apart.

pentagon
A flat shape with five straight sides.

percentage/percent
The number of parts out of a hundred. Percentage is shown by the symbol %.

pi
The circumference of any circle divided by its diameter gives the answer pi. It is represented by the Greek symbol π.

polygon
A 2-D shape with three or more straight sides.

polyhedron
A 3-D shape with faces that are all flat polygons.

positive
A number that is greater than zero.

prime factors
Prime numbers that are multiplied to give a third number. For example, 3 and 5 are the prime factors of 15.

prime number
A number greater than one that can only be divided exactly by itself and one.

probability
The likelihood that something will happen.

product
The answer when two or more numbers are multiplied together.

pyramid
A 3-D shape with a square base and triangular faces that meet in a point at the top.

quadrilateral
A 2-D shape with four straight sides and four angles. Trapeziums and rectangles are both examples of quadrilaterals.

radius
The distance from the center of a circle to its edge.

range
The difference between the smallest and largest numbers in a collection of numbers.

ratio
The relationship between two numbers, expressed as the number of times one is bigger or smaller than another.

right angle
An angle that is exactly 90°.

scalene triangle
A triangle with three different angles and sides that are three different lengths.

sequence
A list of numbers generated according to a rule, for example 2, 4, 6, 8, 10.

square
A 2-D shape with four straight equal sides and four right angles.

squared number
A number multiplied by itself, for example $4 \times 4 = 16$. This can also be written 4^2.

sum
The total, or result, when numbers are added together.

symmetry
A shape or object has symmetry (or is described as symmetrical) if it looks unchanged after it has been partially rotated, reflected, or translated.

table
A list of organized information, usually made up of rows and columns.

tessellation
A pattern of geometric shapes that covers a surface without leaving any gaps.

tetrahedron
A triangular-based pyramid.

theorem
A math idea or rule that has been, or can be, proved to be true.

theory
A detailed, tested explanation of something.

3-D (three-dimensional)
The term used to describe objects that have height, width, and depth.

triangle
A 2-D shape with three straight sides.

2-D (two-dimensional)
A flat object that has only length and width.

velocity
The speed in a direction.

Venn diagram
A method of using overlapping circles to compare two or more sets of data.

vertex (plural vertices)
The corner or point at which surfaces or lines meet within shapes.

vertical
A vertical line runs up and down, at right angles to the horizon.

whole number
A number that is not a decimal or a fraction.

Answers

6-7 A world of math

Panel puzzle
The extra piece is B

Profit margin
Bumper cars: 60 percent of 12 is 7.2
Number of sessions: 4 x 8 = 32
Fares per session: 32 x $2 = $64
$64 x 7.2 = $460.80
Cost to run: $460.80 - $144 = $316.8
Profit: $316.80 per day

A game of chance
There is a 1 in 9 chance of winning:
90 (customers) x 3 (throws) = 270
270 ÷ 30 (coconuts) = 9

12-13 Math skills

Spot the shape
1 D
2 C
3 C
4 C

18-19 Problems with numbers

A useful survey?
1 The survey may be biased because it was carried out by the Association for More Skyscrapers.
2 They only surveyed three of the 30 parks (1 in 10). This is too small a sample to be able to arrive at a conclusion about all the parks.
3 We don't know how many visitors went to the third park.
4 The fact that the other two parks had fewer than 25 visitors all day suggests the survey took place over one day, too short a time frame to draw useful conclusions.

The bigger picture
Because tin helmets were effective at saving lives, more soldiers survived head injuries, rather than dying from them. So the number of head injuries increased, but the number of deaths decreased.

22—23 Seeing the solution

What do you see?
1 Toothbrush, apple, lamp
2 Bicycle, pen, swan
3 Guitar, fish, boat
4 Chess piece, scissors, shoe

Thinking in 2-D

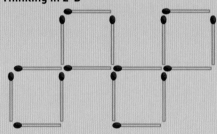

Visual sequencing
Tile 3

Seeing is understanding
The snake is 30 ft (9 m) long.

3-D vision
Cube 2

30-31 Big zero

Roman homework
This question was designed to show why place value makes math so much easier. The quickest way to solve the problem is to convert the numbers and the answer: CCCIX (309) + DCCCV (805) = 1,114 (MCXIV).

34-35 Thinking outside the box

1 Changing places
Second place.
2 Pop!
Use a balloon that's not inflated.
3 What are the odds?
1 in 2.
4 Sister act
They're two of a set of triplets.
5 In the money
Both are worth the same amount.
6 How many?
You would need 10 children.
7 Left or right?
Turn the glove inside out.
8 The lonely man
The man lived in a lighthouse.
9 A cut above
Because it would be more profitable.
10 Half full
Pour the contents of the second cup into the fifth.
11 At a loss
The very rich man started off as a billionaire and made a loss.
12 Whodunnit?
The carpenter, truck driver, and mechanic are all women. Note that the question says fireman, not firefighter.
13 Frozen!
The match!
14 Crash!
Nowhere—you don't bury survivors.
15 Leave it to them
One pile.
16 Home
The house is at the North Pole so the bear must be a white polar bear.

36-37 Number patterns

Prison break
Doors 1, 4, 9 and 16 remain open, so 4 prisoners escape. These are all square numbers. Knowing this pattern, you can quickly work out the answer for 50 guards and 50 prisoners, or even 100.

Shaking hands
3 people = 3 handshakes
4 people = 6 handshakes
5 people = 10 handshakes
The answers are all triangle numbers.

A perfect solution?
The next perfect number is 28. All perfect numbers end in either 6 or 8.

44-45 How big? How far?

Measure the Earth
360° ÷ 7.2° = 50
50 x 500 miles (800 km) = 25,000 miles
(40,000 km).

50-51 Seeing sequences

What's the pattern?
A 1, 100, 10,000, 1,000,000
B 3, 7, 11, 15, 19, 23
C 64, 32, 16, 8
D 1, 4, 9, 16, 25, 36, 49
E 11, 9, 12, 8, 13, 7, 14
F 1, 2, 4, 7, 11, 16, 22
G 1, 3, 6, 10, 15, 21
H 2, 6, 12, 20, 30, 42

52-53 Pascal's triangle

Braille challenge
Look at row 6 of Pascal's triangle and add up the numbers to get 64. This means there are 64 different ways to arrange the dots. For a four-point pattern, go to row 4 of the triangle, which adds up to 16, showing that there are 16 possible ways to arrange the dots.

54-55 Magic squares

Making magic

2	7	6
9	5	1
4	3	8

7	4	9	14
5	11	2	16
10	6	15	3
12	13	8	1

24	18	32	3	11	23
2	25	4	27	22	31
34	9	1	10	36	21
6	26	30	28	5	16
33	14	29	8	20	7
12	19	15	35	17	13

Your own magic square

11	24	7	20	3
17	5	13	21	9
23	6	19	2	15
4	12	25	8	16
10	18	1	14	22

56-57 Missing numbers

Sudoku starter

1	7	6	4	8	9	3	2	5
5	8	9	7	2	3	1	4	6
4	2	3	6	5	1	8	9	7
3	9	2	8	4	7	5	6	1
8	1	4	5	3	6	2	7	9
6	5	7	9	1	2	4	8	3
9	4	5	3	6	8	7	1	2
7	3	1	2	9	4	6	5	8
2	6	8	1	7	5	9	3	4

Slightly harder

7	8	5	6	9	3	1	2	4
9	6	4	5	2	1	3	8	7
2	1	3	8	4	7	6	5	9
3	5	6	7	8	9	2	4	1
8	4	9	2	1	6	5	7	3
1	2	7	3	5	4	8	9	6
5	7	1	9	6	8	4	3	2
4	9	8	1	3	2	7	6	5
6	3	2	4	7	5	9	1	8

Sujiko

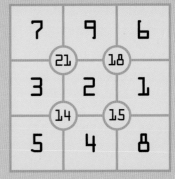

Kakuro

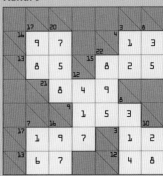

66-67 Puzzling primes

Sifting for primes

1	2	3	4	5	6	7	8	9	10
11	12	13	14	15	16	17	18	19	20
21	22	23	24	25	26	27	28	29	30
31	32	33	34	35	36	37	38	39	40
41	42	43	44	45	46	47	48	49	50
51	52	53	54	55	56	57	58	59	60
61	62	63	64	65	66	67	68	69	70
71	72	73	74	75	76	77	78	79	80
81	82	83	84	85	86	87	88	89	90
91	92	93	94	95	96	97	98	99	100

(Circled primes: 2, 3, 5, 7, 11, 13, 17, 19, 23, 29, 31, 37, 41, 43, 47, 53, 59, 61, 67, 71, 73, 79, 83, 89, 97.)

Prime cubes

123

70-71 Triangles

Measuring areas
The areas of the triangles are:
3 x 7 = 21   21 ÷ 2 = 10.5
3 x 5 = 15   15 ÷ 2 = 7.5
4 x 4 = 16   16 ÷ 2 = 8
4 x 8 = 32   32 ÷ 2 = 16

Add them together:
10.5 + 7.5 + 8 + 16 = 42 square units

80-81 3-D Shape puzzles

Constructing cubes
A + D
H + I
E + G
B + C
F is the odd one out.

Boxing up
Net D will not make a cube.

Face recognition
There are many ways to do this. Here's just one:

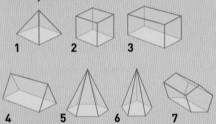

How many more can you find? Experiment with different starting shapes. Also, try making a line of shapes that form a circle.

Trace a trail
You can trace a trail around the octahedron, but not the tetrahedron or cube. This is because the journey is impossible if more than two corners of a shape have an odd number of connections to other corners.

Building blocks
A 10 cm³
B 19 cm³

74-75 Shape shifting

Triangle tally
There are 27 triangles in total.

Tantalizing tangrams

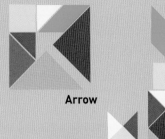

Arrow

Fox

Candle

Shapes within shapes

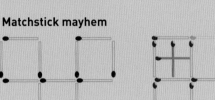

Matchstick mayhem

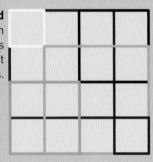

Dare to be square

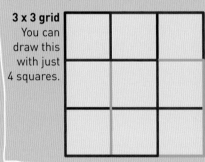

3 x 3 grid
You can draw this with just 4 squares.

4 x 4 grid
You can draw this using just 6 squares.

86-87 Amazing mazes

Simple mazes

Complex mazes

Weave mazes

96-97 Mapping

On the map
Church = 44,01
Campsite = 42,03

100-101 Probability

What are the odds?
The order of likelihood is:
1 Playing soccer
2 Snake bite
3 Falling down a manhole
4 Computer game exhaustion
5 Hippo attack
6 Struck by lightning
7 Hit by a falling coconut
8 Shark attack
9 Walking into a lamppost
10 Hit by a meteorite

104-105 Logic puzzles and paradoxes

Logical square

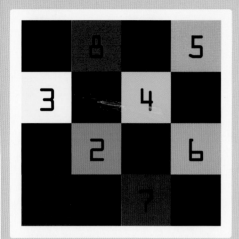

Black or white?

The hat is black. Amy could only know her hat color if both Beth and Claire were wearing white (since she knows that not all three hats are white), but Amy answers "No." That means there must be a black hat on at least one of the others. Beth realizes this and looks at Claire to see if her hat is white, which would mean Beth's was the black one. But it isn't, so Beth answers "No." So Claire must have the black hat, and she knows this because she heard the other sisters' answers.

The barber's dilemma

This story is a paradox.

Four digits

The answer is 1,349.

People with pets

Anna: Nibbles (parrot).
Bob: Buttons (dog).
Cecilia: Snappy (fish).
Dave: Goldy (cat).

Lost at sea

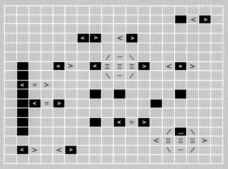

108-109 Codes and ciphers

Caesar cipher

The message reads: "Well done this is a hard code."

Substitution cipher

This message reads: "Codes can be fun."

Polybius cipher

The cipher reads: "This is a very old code."

Shape code

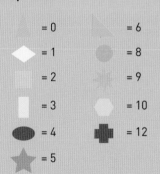

112-113 Algebra

Lunar lightness

Object are six times lighter on the Moon than on the Earth. So, to find out how much you would weigh on the Moon, divide your weight by six.

114-115 Brainteasers

A number of petals

The answer is 117. The pattern is adding up the three smallest numbers, and multiplying the total by the largest number. So (3 + 4 + 6) x 9 = 117.

Cake bake

Jim will need 12 tbsp butter, 1.5 cups sugar, and 3 cups flour.

In a flap

The difference is two. If there were seven birds in the apple tree, for example, and one left to even out the numbers, there would need to be five in the beech tree.

In the balance

You need 12 golf balls.

A fruity challenge

Pineapple = 12
Orange = 18
Apple = 6

Banana = 20
Strawberry = 15
Grapes = 16

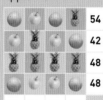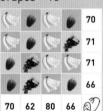

INDEX

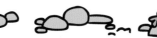

Acknowledgments

DK would like to thank:

Additional editors: Carron Brown, Mati Gollon, David Jones, Fran Jones, Ashwin Khurana

Additional designers: Sheila Collins, Smiljka Surla

Additional illustration: Keiran Sandal

Jacket: Saloni Singh, Priyanka Sharma

Index: Jackie Brind

Proofreading: Jenny Sich

Americanization: John Searcy

The publisher would like to thank the following for their kind permission to reproduce their photographs:

(Key: a-above; b-below/bottom; c-center; f-far; l-left; r-right; t-top)

10-11 Science Photo Library: Pasieka (c) **11 Science Photo Library:** Pascal Goetgheluck (br) **15 Mary Evans Picture Library:** (bl) **16 Getty Images:** AFP (clb). **Science Photo Library:** Professor Peter Goddard (crb). **TopFoto.co.uk:** The Granger Collection (tl) **17 Corbis:** Imaginechina (tr). **Image originally created by IBM**

Corporation: (cl) **18 Science Photo Library:** (bc). **20 Alamy Stock Photo:** Bilwissedition Ltd. & Co. Kg (cr); Dinodia Photos (cla); NASA Image Collection (bl). **21 Alamy Stock Photo:** Imaginechina Limited (tr). **Dreamstime. com:** Grafvision (cb). **Getty Images:** Bettmann (tl); Universal History Archive (clb); Mondadori Portfolio / Hulton Fine Art Collection (clb). **Science Photo Library:** Sheila Terry (cl) **33 akg-images:** (cl). **Corbis:** HO / Reuters (cr). **Science Photo Library:** (c) **38 Getty Images:** AFP (bl) **40 Alamy Images:** Nikreates (cb). **Corbis:** Bettmann (cl); Heritage Images (cr) **41 Getty Images:** Time & Life Pictures (cr, c) **43 NASA:** JPL (br). **Science Photo Library:** Power and Syred (cr) **52 Corbis:** The Gallery Collection (bl) **58 akg-images:** (cr). **Science Photo Library:** (tl); Mark Garlick (bc) **59 akg-images:** Interfoto (br). **Getty Images:** (bc); SSPL (cr). **Mary Evans Picture Library:** Interfoto Agentur (c) **61 Corbis:** ESA / Hubble Collaboration / Handout (br); (bl). **71 Alamy Images:** Mary Evans Picture Library (bl) **73 Corbis:** Jonn / Jonnér Images (c). **Getty Images:** John W. Banagan (cra); Christopher Robbins (tr).

Science Photo Library: John Clegg (cr) **77 Getty Images:** Carlos Casariego (bl) **79 Science Photo Library:** Hermann Eisenbiess (br) **84 Alamy Images:** liszt collection (cl). **TopFoto.co.uk:** The Granger Collection (bl) **85 Corbis:** Bettmann (c); Gavin Hellier / Robert Harding World Imagery (cr). **Getty Images:** (clb) **88 Getty Images:** Juergen Richter (tr). **Science Photo Library:** (bl)**89 Edward H. Adelson:** (br). **Alamy Images:** Ian Paterson (tr) **98 Alamy Stock Photo:** Everett Collection Historical (bl). **Dreamstime.com:** Valya82 (bl/Old book). **Getty Images:** PhotoQuest / Contributor / Archive Photos (cla). **Science Photo Library:** Hagley Museum And Archive (crb). **99 Getty Images:** Bettmann. **110 Getty Images:** Joe Cornish (clb); SSPL (br). **Shutterstock.com:** SherborneSchool / Bournemouth News (tr).**111 Alamy Images:** Pictorial Press (c); Peter Vallance (br). **Getty Images:** SSPL (tr) **116 Dreamstime.com:** Aleksandr Stennikov (cr/Pink Gerbera); Tr3gi (fcr/White Gerbera) **117 Science Photo Library:** Mehau Kulyk (bc) **118 NASA:** (bc,cl). **119 Alamy Stock Photo:** Abaca Press / Olivier Douliery (br). **Getty Images:** Smith Collection / Gado / Contributor / Archive Photos

All other images © Dorling Kindersley
For further information see:
www.dkimages.com